Heart of a Ch

Roberto Duran's last title fight
By
Richard Baker

Copyright Richard Baker - 2013

ISBN - 978-1479372300

Ink & Lens, Ltd

To Brian Halquist – the Northwest's Premier Promoter

Richard Baker is the author of 14 books, winner of the Ernest Hemmingway Award, WBB boxing writer of the year, and sports photographer of the year finalist for American Photo magazine.

Duran's "Hands of Stone" did not destroy his opponents, it was his heart. His fists are legendary: Huertas, Brooks, Wheatley, de Jesus, Kobayashi, Ortiz, Lampkin, and Bizarro – just few in a long list of 70 spectacular knockouts.

I first met Roberto Duran as he sat ringside as a guest at a Patrick Ortiz *Ringside Tickets* boxing event in California. A short fat man with a wide grin covering his face, he looked nothing like the ferocious powerhouse he once was. Maintaining any reasonable weight was often his downfall. He enjoyed the crowd and agreeably signed boxing magazines, posters, gloves, anything to do with boxing. After the fights he posed with patrons in the ring for photographs, always laughing, always willing to bend to any silly pose they requested. He enjoyed the company of people, not just because he was being paid, but because he wanted to be around them. In broken English, he asked as many questions about them as they did about him.

Because I photographed many events for Ortiz I often had the opportunity to see Duran, occasionally in conjunction with Ray Leonard where the two threw mock punches at one another in the ring to an adoring crowd. Once I drove him, his son, and his manager, Tony Gonzales, to the airport several hours after an event. We left about two AM on a rain soaked morning, winding through the California hills. Since I am from Washington, the wet did not concern me but the slick road bothered Duran. He started jabbering to Tony and Tony said Duran wanted me to slow down since I was frightening him. Laughing, I slowed down and gloated at the fact I might have been one of the only men in the world who had actually frightened the greatest lightweight boxer in history.

Some time later, Jeff Connor, who became the ring announcer for the television series *The Contender,* called me from Legends Casino, near Toppenish, Washington. How would I like to be the road manager for Roberto Duran's last fight? I thought I had misunderstood him. Road manager? Roberto Duran? And he is calling me? Yes. Duran wanted to have a fight in his fifth decade and he planned to stage it at Legends Casino against P.J. Goossen during a Patrick Ortiz event. Jeff needed someone to drive him around, purchase and set up his training equipment at various casinos where he would be training, keep his schedule, drive him to events, and make sure he was generally happy. I could hire someone to work with me. Would I do it? I would have been crazy to turn him down. Yes, I was crazy but not that crazy. I took the job. I wanted to know what makes a man a champion and I truly liked Duran, a warm and very human person, no pretense, no superior airs.

Trainer Anthony Hunter came to mind as my assistant. With eight kids Anthony still found time for boxing but enjoyed getting away from the house for a while. When he was not training fighters or at fights he was watching and analyzing videos of fights. Anthony jumped at the chance to join the team.

When Duran made guest appearances at different fights with Sugar Ray Leonard, Leonard was friendly for the contracted time, and then left, while Duran often stayed late into the night and laughed and joked with the patrons. Excess weight had always plagued him throughout his career and he resembled a jolly fat man at these events, eager to laugh. He is a truly honest person who lets his emotions flow easily. There is nothing phony about him and you can believe he is the kind of man who, as champion, stood on the street corners in Panama and gave his earnings away to the poor as they passed by. Leonard, on the other hand, is a businessman and if business requires him to have a smile on his face, then he puts one there, not that it would not be there, anyway. Understanding business is probably the reason Leonard has money and Duran is broke. Duran lives for today; Leonard thinks to the future.

We stood in the baggage section of Sea-Tac International airport waiting for Duran to arrive. I was eager to see him again and his manager Tony Gonzales, a young Florida lawyer excited about boxing. They would not remember me since they meet so many people, and they didn't as they rounded the corner to retrieve their bags. Duran had already lost weight for the fight. Ballooning between fights was common for him. Leonard used the weakness and demanded their second fight take place before Duran could slim back down and get into shape, a smart and business-like move on his part. There are many ways to win a fight and if you cannot beat a man physically, like in their first fight, you must outsmart him for the win. With Duran were his wife, Fulah, and his trainer, Nestor. Connor had said that part of my job was to keep Fulah from arguing with Duran since Duran did not like her along when he fought and she tended to distract him. She did not look friendly as I introduced Anthony and myself. She and Duran had been lovers since childhood and she had put up with his "Macho" ways and his womanizing all these years.

This man seemed a different Duran than the one I knew as a guest at the fights. He had a seriousness about him that I did not recognize. The joking, light-hearted Duran who spent his time charming people, eating and gambling, was much different than the fighting Duran, totally dedicated and concentrated on one goal – to beat an opponent into submission.

Duran has always been an interesting man. He is not a boxer; he is not a puncher; he is a fighter in the pure sense of the word and will box or punch, or gouge, kick, spit, elbow, do anything to win a fight. He was born into abject poverty in Chorrillo, Panama and he often swam to a nearby island to steal mangos and once, while he was swimming back, the heavy load of mangos started dragging him under, but he refused to let go of the sack and almost drowned. Friends pulled him to the surface still grasping the mangos. He sometimes danced on street corners, with local musicians, to earn a few coins and he sold fish he had caught, and shined shoes to make money for the family. Guards, who caught him stealing coconuts from the estate of millionaire Carlos Eleta, brought him before Eleta who sat him down for a long talk. Eleta saw something special in Duran and by that afternoon they had become friends. Eleta later became his manager.

With the help of former national champion, Sammy Medina, Duran found his way into a boxing gym and he turned pro at the age of fifteen in Colon, Panama and knocked out Carlos Mendoza in his first fight. While still a teenager Duran put away future champion Ernesto Marcel then followed that with a sixty-six second knockout of Benny Huertas and wins over Hiroshi Kobayashi and Angel Garcia. These fights set him up for a lightweight title shot against tough Scotsman, Ken Buchanan.

Buchanan was one of the slickest boxers to come from Britain and he had beaten some of the best, including his title win against Ismael Laguna, and had only lost one fight in forty-four matches. Fighting Duran did not bother him. As champion he felt an extra confidence that most challengers do not have. Champions know they are champions. Challengers tend to have a small amount of doubt in their minds and a great amount of hope. Not Duran. He had felt like a champion since his first bout.

Buchanan had never faced anyone as tough as Duran. On the other hand, Duran was not content with beating fighters; he wanted to destroy them, and he didn't care how he did it. During the fight arms, legs, his head, and his fists all were used against Buchanan and after the first few rounds, Buchanan was already a beaten man flinching at every blow. Just the thought of being hit by Duran made him cringe. Finally, in the thirteenth round, Buchanan folded over and onto the canvas holding the jewels between his legs. He claimed he was fouled. Over the years he often changed his story as to how. Sometimes he said Duran had hit him low. At other times he claimed that Duran had kneed him. Some ringsiders attested that he was looking for a way out of the bout. No matter. Duran won by technical knockout when Buchanan refused to continue.

For six-and-a-half years and twelve defenses Duran kept the title by beating such great fighters as Hector Thompson, Ray Lampkin, Ishimatsu Suzuki, Vilomar Fernandez, and Edwin Vireut. On three occasions he fought Puerto Rican Esteban DeJesus losing the first fight, a non-title bout, and winning the next two. By the last fight De-

Jesus had won the WBC title so Duran unified the titles.

Because Duran could not maintain his weight, he vacated the titles to move to welterweight. A string of bright stars waited for him there: Sugar Ray Leonard, Wilfred Benitez, Pipino Cuevas, Thomas Hearns, and Carlos Palomino. After beating Carlos Palomino, Duran signed to face champion Sugar Ray Leonard in a bout that brought in more than 47,000 fans to Olympic Stadium. Leonard made the mistake of trying to fight with Duran, a bad move because in a real fight, Duran was unbeatable. All a man could do was outsmart him, not out-brawl him. Duran won the fight. In their next fight Leonard taunted Duran, tried to humiliate and disrespect him. Duran, who couldn't understand why Leonard refused to fight like a man, finally uttered those famous words, "no mas, no mas." Referee Octavio Meyran thought he had misunderstood, but he didn't. Duran had quit. During our time together I attempted to find out the real reason he quit since it has been a great mystery in boxing. He seldom talked about that night. Sometimes he gave the standard answer that he was sick and had an upset stomach. Once he said there was no use trying to fight someone who wouldn't fight and he thought it was beneath him to chase around a coward.

Duran, once hero to the people of Panama, was now a disgrace and he quickly learned how fickle fight fans are. Former fans wanted nothing to do with him yet he fought on, trying to regain their respect. He moved to Jr. middleweight and lost twice to Wilfred Benitez, then to Englishman Kirkland Laing, hardly a household word in boxing. He seemed all but finished before Top Rank gave him one last chance against Cuevas. Against all predictions, Duran kayoed him, earning him a shot at WBA champ Davy Moore. Now 32 years old, Duran entered the ring a five-to-two underdog. Again he didn't seem to have a chance yet, from the opening round he battered Moore around the ring, closing his eye early and putting him away in round eight to win the championship. Now, up against Marvin Haggler, he staged a great fight but age was catching up with him and he ran out of gas toward the end and lost a unanimous decision. Thomas Hearns was next in line. It was not Duran's night as Hearns knocked him out for the first time in his life. Certainly he was finished now but one of the reasons I admired him so much was his refusal to quit. He had guts, the one thing a boxer needed most.

Once again he carried the mangos across the water. After losing to Robbie Sims, he won his next five in a row and, at the age of 37, earned a shot at WBC champ Iran Barkley. No one had money on Duran. Barkley was simply too slick. Yet, Duran dropped Barkley in round eleven and won a split decision.

Now, at the age of 50, he was in Washington to win one more title against P.J. Goossen at Legends Casino, nothing big, just a little alphabet title that meant little to him except he could sell the belt to help ease his constant financial problems and he could be back in the ring and pound on someone later, anyway.

The drive to Rochester and the Lucky Eagle Casino, his first stop on the training tour, was quiet and I tried to make conversation but no one was interested except Tony. Tony is affable with a wide smile and large bright eyes and he told me of his involvement with his newest prospect, Six Head Lewis, a fighter who did not impress me. Duran sat quietly in the front seat staring at the evening sky and I wondered what a man like him thought about while training. Certainly, after all his fights, another battle could not have the same intensity as the earlier ones. I know he needed money but was that all there was to it? The plane had arrived late and I rushed to the casino an hour-and-a-half away. Fulah remained reticent in the backseat and there was a certain amount of tension in the van. Had they been fighting?

Duncan McLeod met us at the casino where a ring had been rented for Duran to stand and meet the people. Duncan said he would drive Duran and Tony to the Quinault Casino, the next stop, if I wanted to take Fulah there now so she could rest. They had a room reserved and they were to stay there several days as he trained and ran along the beach. During the drive I managed to get a word or two from her but nothing more. I became determined to loosen up the group so we could all be civilized. After arriving at the casino she immediately rushed to her suite, a two-room affair with fireplace overlooking the Pacific Ocean. Anthony and I had our own room with a fireplace and ocean view.

Tony said they would be running at 6 AM so we met them downstairs the following morning. I had my camera and Duran smiled and seemed to warm a little. Tony was good-natured as always even though he did not care to be up that early. Duran wore a sweat suit and a knit hat with Mickey Mouse on the front. They started the run by doing laps in the fog around the parking lot as we stood with trainer Nestor Quinonies. Anthony and Nestor hit it off immediately and started talking about fighters and training. Nestor's English was rough but they conversed by demonstrating with punches thrown in the air and against each other. They got wrapped up in an explanation of the "goncho" punch and how it was delivered. There is some swampland around the casino with a long entrance road through the marsh and Tony and Duran took off down the road. Twenty minutes later, when they returned, an exhausted Tony, said, "That's enough for today." Duran looked at him and shook his head, then trotted off around the parking lot and down the road again. He never looked for a reason to quit or to go easy on himself.

"He wears me out," Tony said. "He's fifty years old and won't stop."

I was beginning to learn what makes a champion. It was almost impossible to get any of the local fighters to do roadwork and it was Anthony's biggest complaint. He felt they were lazy and that is why they would not go any farther than club fights. Still, they wanted to be treated like champions. When Duran returned he passed quietly and kept going, not stopping for another twenty minutes. They then returned to their rooms while Anthony and I started setting up the equipment.

Bear, an Indian from the Quinault Reservation, a top trainer and cut man, had supplied the ring and set it up in the empty bingo room. A thin man with sharp features, he runs an amateur boxing program on the reservation and trained heavyweight contender, Joe Hipp. He can be seen at almost every Northwest fight working corners as a cut man. The Quinault maintenance staff helped build a special collapsible stand for the speed bag and also hung the heavy bag from a rafter.

The promoter, Patrick Ortiz, was nowhere to be seen. He is a young promoter and very good at what he does although he is sometimes not business oriented. Much of the tour he was absent, usually jogging or doing laps in the pool – he is in very good shape- and tending to his personal affairs. The casino manager had many questions and at first I didn't know what to say except that Patrick would eventually be along. When he didn't show up I started answering the questions as if I were in charge. Once that was established, the rest of the tour was easy.

Over breakfast Anthony and I discussed some of Duran's fights and talked about he and Tony and Nestor and Fulah. Duran seemed full of fight, very determined, unlike when he was on his autograph signing tours constantly smiling and playing to the crowds. Tony grinned all the time and it was impossible not to like him. He was instantly everyone's friend. Nestor was also personable, long, old and lanky and quick to share boxing secrets unlike most trainers. Fulah never made an appearance.

The bingo room filled up that afternoon as people waited to see Duran work out. Young boxers from the reservation appeared with wide and shy eyes. A few old men lounged on nearby chairs and several women, curious about the fuss, stood drinking coffee. Duran entered the room, wearing a sour look like a dog not to be petted, and immediately slid between the ropes and started throwing punches and moving around the ring. All business, he paid no attention to anyone, his punches landing on the air as if he had a real opponent in front of him. From the ring he moved to the speed bag, a device we soon learned he hated. He did not believe the bag built timing or speed or coordination and he looked upon it as a nuisance. He did not have the timing or rhythm he once had and the bag refused to cooperate, often flopping at odd angles and refusing a steady beat. Frustration built up in his eyes. From there he moved to the heavy bag, something he did like and something he understood. A sparring partner was supposed to have been arranged but so far no one had shown. Duran crushed the heavy bag as it doubled over and swayed and he enjoyed sinking his fists deep into something tough and making the bag surrender. The more the bag twirled and dimpled and rocked the more he liked it.

Tony asked about the sparring partner. I didn't know. Ortiz said one would be supplied but I should have known better. The only things that get taken care of are the ones you do and if Ortiz had asked me I would have supplied a sparring partner. I would not make the mistake again. But the crowd wanted to see Duran in the ring with someone, anyone. I asked Bear if he knew of anyone nearby. His fighters were all kids and we were a long way from any town. Finally Anthony stepped up and said he would spar with Duran. I was surprised. Sparring with Duran could be dangerous and I did not know if Anthony had ever boxed. Anthony knew the crowd wanted to see Duran in the ring with someone and he was willing to throw himself on the grenade.

I crated Anthony in headgear and laced up the gloves. His eyes shown large and he kept watching Duran in the opposite corner. I had seen that look before, just before men had gone into battle and weren't sure they would survive. Duran banged his gloves together and I asked Tony to tell Duran to go easy. At the bell Duran advanced as Anthony moved to the side. Soon they were at it and Duran did take it easy. He banged Anthony around for two minutes as Anthony grunted and groaned at each blow but it all ended when Duran caught him with a hard left hook against the side of the head.

Anthony yelled out, "Oh no! Oh no!" His arms flung through the air like tails on a kite and he staggered against the ropes. Catching himself, he stumbled around the ring saying, "That's it. I've had enough."

Duran stood; his arms at his sides, with a stupefied look on his face. He asked Tony if Anthony had ever boxed before, had ever been in the ring with anyone even as an amateur. Anthony confessed he had never boxed but the crowd had wanted to see Duran hit someone and he was trying to oblige. When Tony explained the situation to Duran, he laughed and walked up to Anthony and, in English, said, "Hit me. Hit me and you will feel better. I will stand here with my hands down and you just hit me." He picked up Anthony's fists and banged himself in the face with them. "Come, hit me; hit me hard." When Anthony refused he threw his arms around Anthony and smiled for the first time on the tour. He rubbed Anthony on the head and, to the crowd, said, "My good friend," and we all started laughing including the crowd who did not quit understand what had happened. Everything changed from that point on. Because of Anthony we were now part of the family and I was included. We became inseparable for the rest of the tour, eating together, talking together, shopping together, training together, and spending our spare time together.

Several days later we left the smells of ocean salt air and drove to Tacoma. We dropped Duran and his crew at the motel and went to the Emerald Queen Casino to prepare the afternoon's workout. The Casino, owned by the Puyallup tribe of Indians, earned a great amount of money and, under the direction of Frank Wright, an easy-going man who had always supported my projects, remained generous and freely contributed to the city and to their people. The casino had a riverboat, a building on shore, and a large tent for entertainment. The plan was to later build a new casino near the freeway and a new entertainment center and a hotel. Those projects have since been completed.

The ring had already been erected and we placed the other equipment nearby. Avoiding any further problems, I had arranged two sparring partners to alternate on different days. The first had been Candy Robertson, managed by Mike Morton. Mike's fighter Ray Lampkin had almost beaten Duran in Panama and I thought he might like to talk to Duran again. The other boxer was Brock Stodden from Bremerton, once trained by three-time lightweight champion, Greg Haugen. He had some skills but one terrible flaw – a glass jaw. Almost always ahead in his fights, he would catch a punch and go down and usually out. It was so bad that the Washing State licensing division, in an effort to save his life, had revoked his license. He took them to court and won it back, the court deciding a man can kill himself if he wants to in a sport, just not in the privacy of his own bedroom.

We picked up Duran that afternoon and presented him to a small crowd sitting around the ring. He went right to work. People in the crowd asked me questions and I answered as best I could as I waited for Robertson and Morton. They finally showed an hour after their scheduled time. When I asked where they had been, Robertson, always full of himself, said "We work at our own time, not his." He shot a nasty glance at Duran as if he were the *nobody* sparring partner and not him.

Robertson had always been a disappointment to Morton, no discipline, yet with potential. He generally knocked out poor handpicked opponents, who only added to his ego and he started to believe his own press. He had few skills except a punch and he refused to listen to any trainer, claiming he had his own style and he was sticking with it. A natural athlete, he seldom trained and seldom did little road work. Any fight lasting more than four rounds exhausted him but with proper training he might have become a contender instead of someone who will spend his life in anonymity. Arrogance is man's greatest destroyer and Morton, now in a wheel chair, so wanted a champion that he put up with Robertson in hopes he might change. Hope might be eternal but life is not. Morton never got that champion and died a few years later, a true gentleman respected by almost everyone.

Entering the ring to warm up, Robertson refused to acknowledge Duran until they were brought together in the center of the ring. He never intended to spar because he had something to prove; he wanted to knock Duran out and he started throwing his hardest punches and tried to shove Duran around. One of his punches, one he knew would take Duran out, landed right on Duran's chin but Duran, once he realized what was happening, just smiled and came ahead and knocked him all over the ring and made him look just like what he was, a rank amateur with big mouth. The crowd loved the tussle and after several rounds Robertson was exhausted while Duran looked like a kid. After the sparring I told Morton we didn't need Robertson back. He understood. Robertson huffed away, leaving Morton to wheel himself out.

Duran likes a good fight and he was now in a terrific mood and actually took time to converse with the crowd and to sign pictures and autographs as they gathered around him, as they might any idol. Most of them were afraid to speak as if talking would ruin the moment. Duran smacked the speed bag one time on his way out and we drove him to the motel to clean up before returning to the casino for dinner.

Man, can Duran eat! It had been his downfall in the second Leonard fight and he often put on fifty pounds or more between fights. We ate in the light-filled restaurant overlooking the riverboat and people glanced our way, probably because we looked out of place, casually dressed in a rather formal place. Duran wore his Mickey Mouse hat. While most people were quiet, and trying to decide who we were, we were loud and Tony and Nestor laughed, speaking Spanish, Anthony carrying his big grin, even Duran grunting out a chuckle or two between mouthfuls. Duran piled on the food, two steaks, two baked potatoes, two plates to hold the salad and vegetables. He said he needed the food to train and he worked the calories off each day. Besides, compared to what he normally ate, he was almost on a diet.

Whispers started creeping around the room as eyes pointed our way, a glance here, a look there, gentle whispers between a tall white-haired man and his chubby wife, her chins doubled under her neck. A former world champion was in the room. Someone had noticed him, an old fan perhaps. Who would make the first move, the white-haired man, maybe the man in the plaid shirt with the beard? No, it was actually a woman in a blue dress as she slapped her husband for being such a coward, then moved our way with a pen she had taken from her leather purse, and a napkin.

"Are you Roberto Duran?" she said. "My husband said you are and that you were one of the greatest fighters there ever was." She twiddled with the pen and shifted her weight from one leg to the other. Duran forced a smile, signed the napkin before diving back into the food like a wolf with a fresh kill. Soon another person came up, and then another until a small line had formed. He signed everything, but not happily since he did not enjoy people coming between him and his food.

I made arrangements for the following day's run at a quiet little track in a park not far from my house. He wanted to go at 5 AM so he could get some sleep afterwards so I called the sparring partner's manager to make sure everything was on for the afternoon's session. He said Brock would be there. Everyone liked Brock Stodden and he was especially appreciated in Bremerton, his hometown, a navy town filled with new and old ships crammed onto its harbor. He worked in construction, had a fine family and looked great in his green boxing robe and white shoes. He loved boxing and couldn't get enough of fighting. As much as Candy Robertson didn't work or listen, Stodden worked very hard perfecting the craft and welcoming all advice. Fate had done him a dirty trick giving him that glass jaw and taking away the one thing he loved, outside his family. People attempted to get him out of boxing through concern, not spite.

The following morning, with all of us sleepy, we drove quietly to the park, Duran in his Mickey Mouse hat, Tony in sweats. I sat on a bench with my camera as they took off slowly into the mist. I left part of my hip in Vietnam so running is out of the question, not that I like to run, anyway. I am quite content to sit and take pictures of other people in strenuous situations. Tony and Duran finished their first lap. Tony was only good for one other lap and he dropped out beside me to take a breather. Duran never stopped his stride and jogged around three or four more times. He seemed to have endless energy while I became tired just taking pictures. I had never seen a person, at any age, so determined.

That afternoon we entered the casino to find Brock Stodden waiting with his trainer. Eager to meet Duran he held out an anxious hand and said, "This is an honor. You have always been one of my heroes and I am glad I get to work with you." Duran shook his hand and slapped him on the shoulder. Stodden is a left-hander and Duran asked him if he would turn conventional. Stodden was happy to try, anything for the champ. After a brief warm-up they entered the ring as Stodden gave Duran good work, but, once, Duran caught him with a decent left hook and Stodden, with his glass jaw, almost went down. Later on Duran fired a nice hard right that caught Stodden on the top of the head. Duran seemed to wince and quickly drew back his hand. They sparred another round and when they had finished Duran placed his arms around Stodden and said what a good man he was and that he wanted to work with him again. Stodden grinned widely and said he had difficulty with the conventional style but he hoped everything had worked out OK.

Duran, to the delight of the onlookers, spent another twenty minutes on the heavy bag. He continued to hit the bag with tremendous force as if it were someone he had caught sleeping with his wife. Afterwards he spoke quietly to Tony showing him his little finger. Tony felt it and shook his head.

"He thinks he broke his little finger on Stodden's head," he said. "We will have to get the thing checked out."

Sure enough the finger was broken, a hairline fracture running the length of one of the bones. There was no reason to cast it and the finger stood bent at a strange angle. I thought that, after all this training, all this publicity, the fight would be called off.

"Do you want me to call Patrick and let him know?" I said.

"No, no," Tony said. "It's nothing."

"A broken finger is nothing?" I said. Tony looked at Duran for help.

"Always I break something," Duran said. "The finger has been broken many times and still I fight. Always something is hurt; a muscle, a …" he pointed to his knee, "a shoulder or knuckle. It's nothing. I am a fighter and I don't cry. I just fight and the hurt makes me fight more." I wanted to get inside the head of a real champion. Now, I was starting to understand. Duran was complicated in a simple sort of way. Fearless, able to absorb pain and use the pain to his advantage, he also respected other fighters and other people in a way more sensitive than I had imagined.

I often think of Duran and laugh at all the fighters who winge about every little ache and bruise. I still remember Greg Haugen tearing the ligaments in his right shoulder in the first round of a fight against Paul Nave in California. Haugen's trainer, Victor Machado, wanted to stop the fight. Haugen said, "No way. I can beat this punk with one hand." Champions make no excuses.

They decided to take the following day off and visit Seattle and see Pike's Place Market, an old farmer's market on the seedy side of town along First Avenue with the peep shows and prostitutes, winos and bums. They also wanted to find a Chinese pharmacy for an ointment to put on the finger. Duran is a great believer in folk medicines, especially from the Orient, and, perhaps because of his childhood, prefers them to conventional medicine.

Seattle's China Town is minute compared to San Francisco's, a smattering of businesses sprinkling the south side of town near the site of the old Kingdome and we parked outside an Asian market and entered a pharmacy across the street. Duran wore a black leather coat given to him by the Emerald Queen Casino and he had brought

Fulah with him, the first time we had seen her since they had gotten here. With Tony's help he managed to convey his wishes to the girl behind the counter who had no idea who he was. She was far too young and since there are no great Chinese boxers she would have had no interest in the sport. She produced several vials of ointment that Duran smelled and felt as he looked at his broken finger, pulled on it, and attempted to stretch out the kink. Finally, deciding on a bottle, he rubbed the ointment around the finger, pulled it by the end, pointed it toward Tony and me, and smiled as if he had discovered a precious jewel. He lingered in the store fingering different items and checking them for quality before leaving.

He was not long at Pike's Place Market before being recognized. Several people glanced his way, whispered quietly to their companions, and pointed fingers before a group of three males came his way. One of them finally said, "We don't mean to interrupt, but are you Roberto Duran?" As if they already knew the answer, one of the men produced a napkin and a pen for an autograph. Since this was Duran's day off, he grinned and gladly nodded and signed the paper. Other people noticed the gathering and the signing and quickly word spread until a fairly significant group gathered. Since he had not been in the spotlight for a long time, it was amazing how many people knew him. Being a champion often means never being alone. Having patience is a great asset. Even people who did not know him knew his name and wanted his autograph so they could boast to their friends about meeting him. After several minutes Duran grew tired of the notoriety and turned rather sour. He shook his hands in the air and started to walk off toward the fish being tossed around inside the building and pinched the brightly colored fruits and vegetables, leaving the crowd to stare behind on the street.

Downstairs he seemed to be fascinated with a giant shoe in a window, supposedly the biggest shoe ever made. On the wall was the picture of another shoe, about eight feet long, and an eyepiece one could peer through to see a small movie about the shoe. Duran looked through the eyepiece and I thought, what a great shot it was but he turned away before I got it. I didn't want to let it go so I asked if he would look in the eyepiece again so I could get a shot of him and the shoe. He looked annoyed as if he had already accommodated everyone enough. I said it was a photographic joke; that in the U.S. a man with the biggest feet had the biggest sex organ so he should be photographed with the biggest shoe. He laughed and went back to the eyepiece where he stood until I got my shot. He continued to tour the area with Tony at his side and Fulah and me walking behind like two stray puppies. When he was no longer amused, we left to prepare to travel to Yakima on the following day.

Yakima (or Yakama as the Indians spell it) in Eastern Washington is the complete opposite of Western Washington: dry and barren compared to wet and green. Legends Casino is a little oasis in Toppenish, in the middle of the desert and owned by the Yakima Indians. Jeff Connor effectively ran the media section of the casino, often by browbeating his young assistant, Shawn Haggerty. Connor and Haggerty booked shows and brought in crowds and Connor had a soft spot for lost souls.

They had set us up at a fine hotel in Yakima, twenty miles from the casino that had a bicycle and walking track beside the river. Arrangements had been made for him to train at a local gym and Duran wanted to visit the facilities and also bounce around the ring at Toppenish. Fulah stayed in the room as we left. He was very happy with the gym as he walked through and swung the bags, punching several before smacking the speed bag with contempt before leaving.

The crew had erected the fight ring outside the Casino on a parking lot. Duran swung between the ropes, his face serious as if he already had an opponent before him. He slid around the ring jabbing, hooking, throwing uppercuts, his face an iron mask and he looked like a young man, extremely fast, and he was throwing so hard Anthony and I were sure he would knockout Goossen. I had never seen an old man with such energy and power.

The following morning we were met with a video camera. One of the producers from a new national sports show, *Beyond the Glory*, was there to do a story on Duran so he started filming immediately. After seeing me take pictures he struck up a conversation and soon asked if I wanted to be the still photographer for the Duran story.

They eventually used eighteen of my pictures in the episode, more photos from a single photographer than on any other show. Duran, used to such media attention, paid the crew no mind and acted as if they were not there.

At the gym that afternoon he drew a large audience, especially young boxers lining the walls like bug-eyed insulation. The casino had provided him with a long white limousine, a suite at the best hotel, and he was living in style, although he would have been happy in a shack .The gym had no air conditioning and he felt at home, as if he were back in Panama, and he seemed to enjoy the sweat running down his neck and back leaving stains on his sweat suit. He immediately went to the heavy bag, surrounded by full-length mirrors, and banged away for half an hour.

Next came the sparring as the crowd gathered closer. One man, a little heavy-set, remained in the background almost unnoticed, standing by the door during the session. I watched him mill nervously and something seemed wrong so I kept my eye on him should he start any trouble. After the sparring Duran held up his hands and paraded around the ring as everyone applauded. Nestor removed his gear and people started handing him papers to be autographed. He signed several on his way to the limousine, but, just as he ducked into the car, the heavy-set man handed him an envelope as if he wanted the paper signed. He then shouted, "You've been served! Roberto Duran, you've been served!" The envelope came flying back out the window. I was not sure what was happening but I immediately stood on the envelope.

The big guy grabbed my leg, the bad one injured in the war, and tried to lift it to get the subpoena. I moved the leg around holding down the paper as the big guy chased after my foot. He grabbed my leg again and wrenched the knee and I smacked him on the forehead and he fell over backwards.

"Don't go grabbing my body," I said.

He gave me a nasty look and jumped at me again and attempting to lift the leg. I grabbed him by the shoulders, lifted him and threw him against a tree where he slithered down to the ground. He rolled over and ran down the driveway and around the corner shouting, "You've been served! You've been served!"

The white limousine pulled quietly away and out of sight.

People with a reputation and money are constantly being sued. Duran had, at least, the reputation, and he was usually being sued for taking money and not paying back the loan or, in this case, borrowing money on his house and not making repayment. Now the lender wanted the house.

That afternoon I met Pat Goossen and his son P.J., Duran's opponent. P.J. brushed back his blond hair and seemed excited and energized about the fight and confident he could win. I rode in their limo back to the gym for their workout. I knew Pat was a Vietnam veteran, just the way he acted, the tinge of sadness and despair about him and that thousand mile stare that vets have as if looking into nothing and into the souls of everything all at the same time, the good and evil and all the questions that can't be answered in this world and maybe not in the next. That night, since we were both unable to sleep, we met outside in the warm air jacketed with coolness. Like many vets he had been self-medicating, drowning his pain with liquor.

"Been to Nam," I asked him?

"Yeh," he said.

"Me, too."

We never mentioned it again because nothing further had to be said, the "Yeh" said everything, brought back all the images, the feelings, the smells of napalm, cordite, diesel fuel and burning shit. I liked him right away and hoped he might eventually overcome the pain. Several years later, when his other son died in a car accident, he refused to train P.J. because he refused to be responsible for him getting hurt.

The weigh-in was a gala affair packed with local reporters and tribal members. Raphael, one of the world's best cut men, had shown up and he and Anthony had gotten into a rousing discussion. Raphael wore his trademark taxicab hat covered with pins from around the world. Duran is so attuned to his body that he knew exactly what he weighed before he even stepped onto the scale, remarkable considering I had never seen him weigh himself the whole time we were together. He said what he weighed; he stepped onto the scale and clinched his arms together like a muscle man;

and that is what he weighed. He paid no attention to P.J., not even to look at him with disdain or any other feeling. P.J. made weight with no problem, two real professionals and not like many of the clowns seen today constantly missing weight. Duran gathered up Tony and took him to see Anthony as Tony interpreted.

"Duran says you are a good man," Tony said. Duran grinned. "He wants you to work his corner and to carry in his championship belt and parade the belt around the ring at the beginning of the fight."

Anthony looked overwhelmed and was speechless. He stood to shake Duran's hand.

"A good man," Duran said, pumping Anthony's hand like the handle of an outdoor well.

After the weigh-in, Duran immediately scurried to the buffet in the casino. He started at one end of the counter with several plates and piled them high all the way to the other. Anthony and I were not sure that was a good idea, especially when he went back for more. That afternoon, as we sat in the hot tub, we discovered he had returned for even more food and then, when he got back to the hotel, he went to the restaurant across the parking lot for cake, pie, and ice cream. A lot of hard work was about to disappear.

Sparse clouds glowed blood red as the setting sun lit the preliminary bouts the night of the fight. The night started to transform into a purple-blue before the main event. During the break before Duran's fight, I visited him in the dressing room. Few people talked in the room and those that did spoke in whispers as the *Beyond The Glory* cameraman moved slowly to record the historic event. Anthony stood in one corner with his arms crossed, his hat tipped back and looking much like Floyd Patterson. Raphael sat on a chair in another corner while Nestor taped Duran's hands. Duran had been soaking his broken finger and hand in a bucket of ice water. Fulah paced nervously near-by. Duran wore nothing but his underwear, groin protector, and green handmade boxing shoes and he looked visibly much heavier than before the weigh-in.

He stood before a full-length mirror and started throwing punches, to warm up. His lightning-fast punches seemed much slower and he plodded rather than floated and he looked nothing like the man who had been training the last few weeks. I looked at Anthony and asked him about the problem. Duran had eaten himself into lethargy. He could not modify himself for just one more day to retain some of the old glory. I walked back to the apron outside, disappointed and disillusioned because I had such hope in him, because I knew if he could overcome age then I could overcome my illness from the war. The knockout I knew was coming would not be there, that last grasp at youth gone. The Duran of old I had envisioned was old, a half-century old, old and plodding the result of several pounds of baked potatoes piled high with gravy, smothered in pork dressing, the blood of four half-raw steaks turning the plate red. Overeating at this stage seemed a stupid mistake for such a smart fighter but I think it was a result of his youth. He had been so deprived, so poor as a kid, had gone hungry so many times that he wanted everything now, all the food to prove to himself that he would never go hungry again, that if nothing else lasted he would always have a good meal. Food was his heroin, his mistress, his salvation and his god. He was not eating just for himself, he was eating for all the starving poor in all the world and he ate as hard as he fought because he wanted it all, all the glory, all the championships, all the food, but perhaps he realized that, at his age, only the food remained. P.J. Goossen now had a chance to beat one of the greats, to out-speed him and, because P.J. had longer arms, work him from the outside, building up points and cutting him apart.

Fireworks streaked and burst through the night air like an artillery barrage singling the main event and the arrival of Duran. The crowd rose to its feet making a small corridor for him to enter. A yellow searchlight path marked the pavement as the entourage stepped on the light and marched forward with Anthony leading the way flashing the championship belt above his head like a prize salmon. Duran walked slowly, his head down, arms at his side, his face looking as if it were attempting to solve a complicated algebra problem. P.J. had entered almost unnoticed a few minutes earlier, no fanfare, no spotlight, just him and his father sliding through the ropes to do a job. He looked pale and tough in his dark corner, his blond hair slightly spiked, and sweat covering his body from a good warm-up.

Both men came out hard at the bell, both swinging, neither looking for a feeling-out round, just wanting to get things over, each trying to establish himself, to show he was the man in charge, the man of the hour. P.J. smacked Duran some vicious shots. Duran was never one to avoid punishment and his head rocked from side to side with the blows, each time righting itself with a vicious little grin across his face. He fired back but the slow punches mostly missed or, those that landed, did little damage. The crowd remained ecstatic, roaring at each blow Duran landed and he seemed to land more as the fight continued. His timing slowly returned and he appeared to be fighting himself back into shape. His punches became faster as the fight continued and, although he mostly plodded ahead, he appeared less heavy, not floating exactly, not at all light on his feet, but like a heavy man who had just dropped a bag of potatoes and now left a lighter impression in the sand. P.J. still pounded him badly but the blows left no mark, no imprint, only rocked Duran's head as if his head were supposed to rock. And, as the bout continued, Duran became stronger while Goossen grew weaker and started throwing fewer punches. Punches that were hard but ineffective eventually became defective, meaningless pats and punches piddled out as afterthoughts.

Goossen, although exhausted, hung on until the end. The decision was not in doubt and as Duran's hand was raised, the crowd went wild and people crowded the ring as Anthony paraded around holding the belt high overhead. TV lights glared and reporters and photographers were drawn in by Duran's gravitational pull as the rest of his solar system orbited gleefully around the ring. At the age of 50, Duran was again champion.

No one becomes a world champion boxer without dedication. Most fighters cannot retain that dedication much past the age of 30. Those that do have already started to deplete their physical skills. Only a fighter with an exceptional heart can continue. Roberto Duran and Archie Moore fought nearing the age of 50. At that age, Duran trained to fight for the WBF World Title. The determination needed by a young man to fight for any title is exceptional; for an old man, almost impossible.

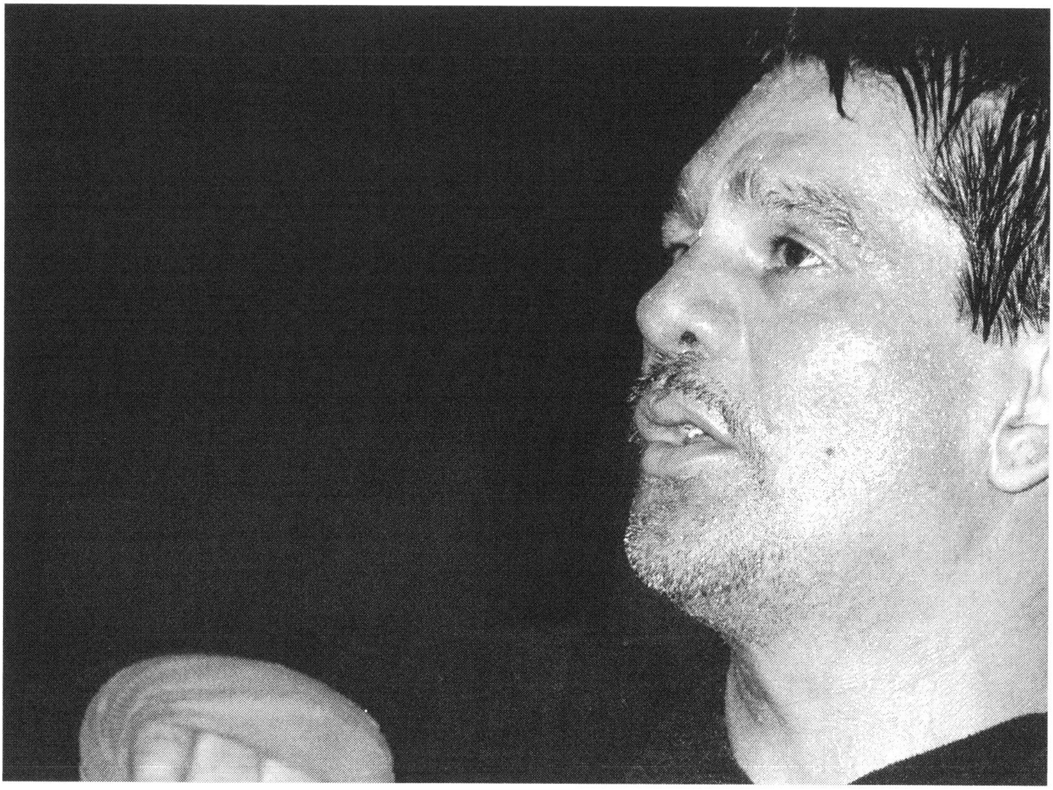

A snappy dresser at events, he is often more comfortable wearing jeans and sweatshirts. Here he sits opposite Sugar Ray Leonard at an event. He has always liked Leonard and considers him a very smart man.

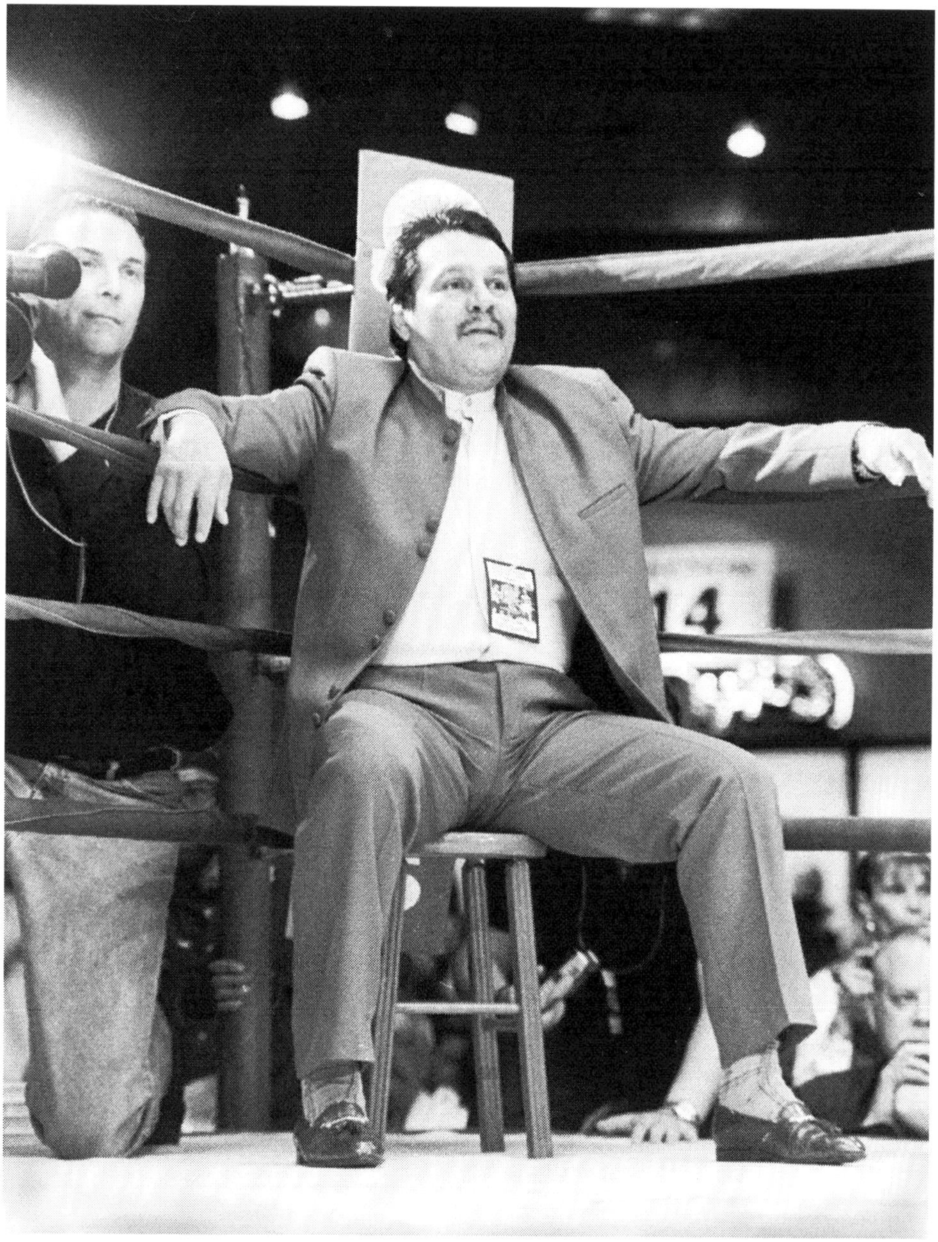

Duran is willing to attempt any pose to please his fans. He enjoys people, especially women. He also enjoys a good party and friends.

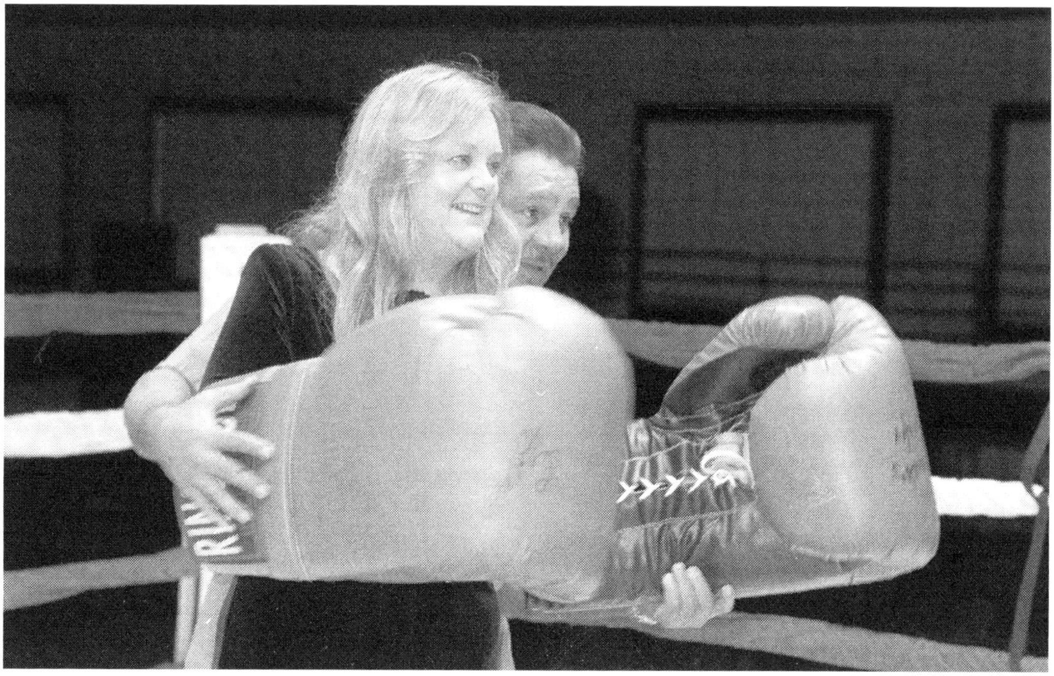

He is gracious with Leonard at events and always gives him praise in the ring. Leonard accepts the praise well.

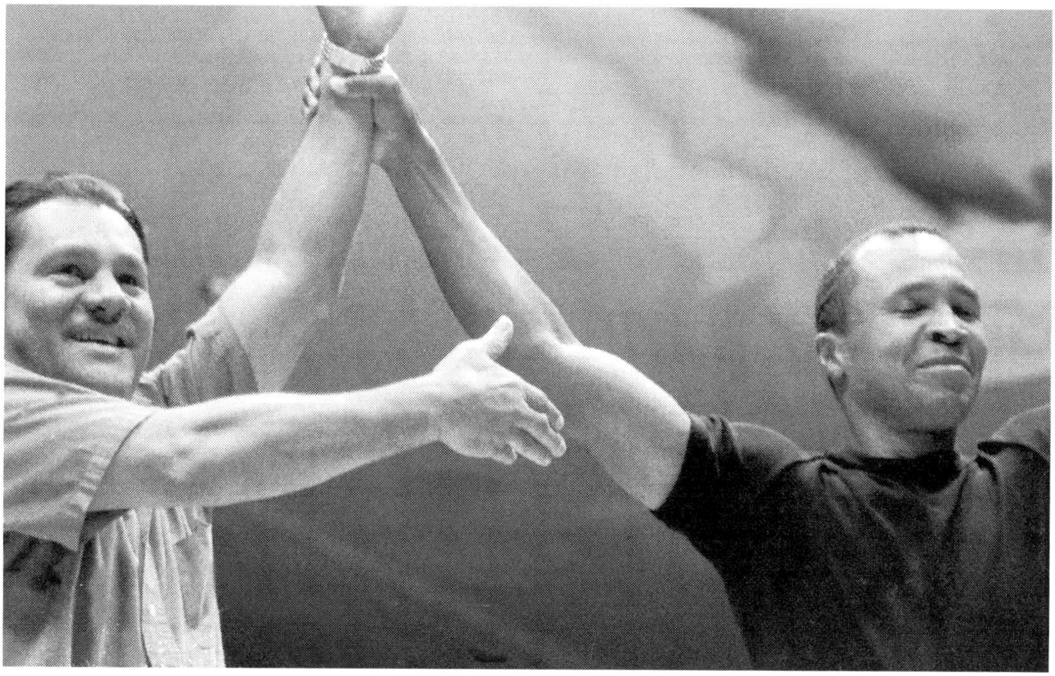

Duran gathers his thoughts at a press conference. He is aware that his English is not that good so he tries to put a few sentences in order before he speaks.

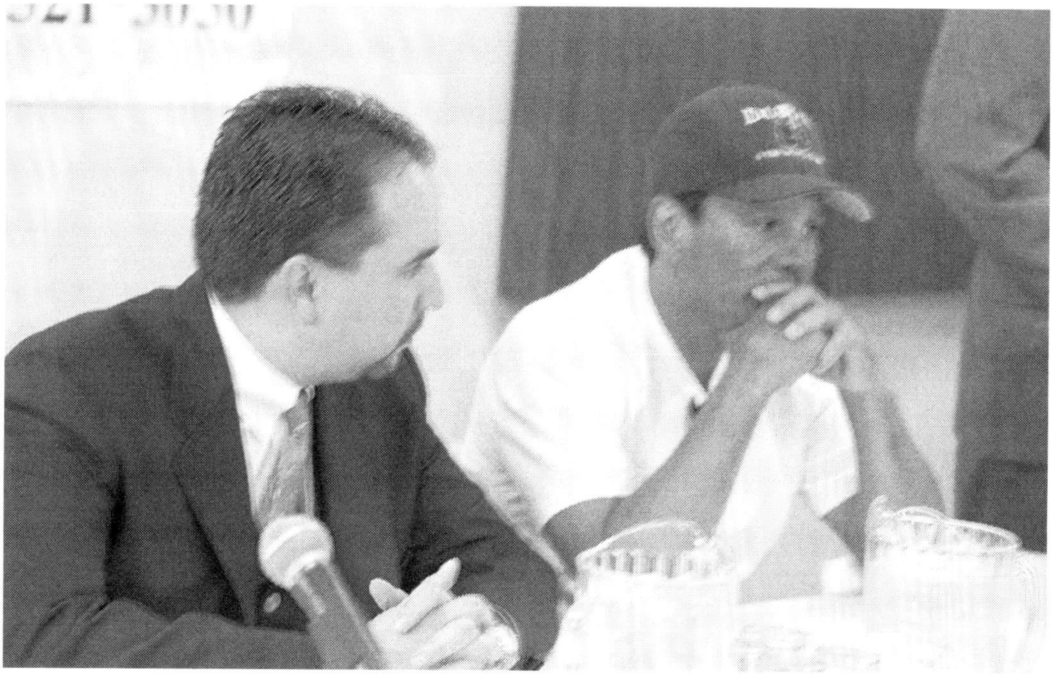

At the microphone he turns on the charm. He has an appealing smile and bright, child-like eyes. In the ring the smile turns to grimace, the eyes, to malice.

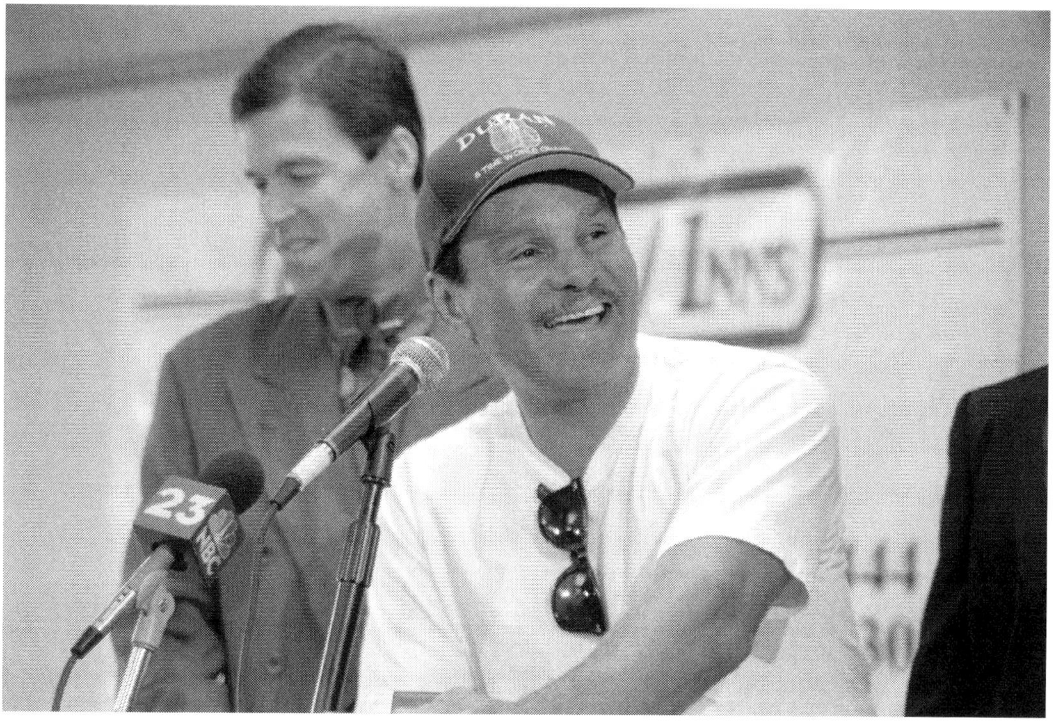
DURAN
23
NBC

In the gym in California, Pat Goossen talks to brother, Joe, about the upcoming fight with Duran.

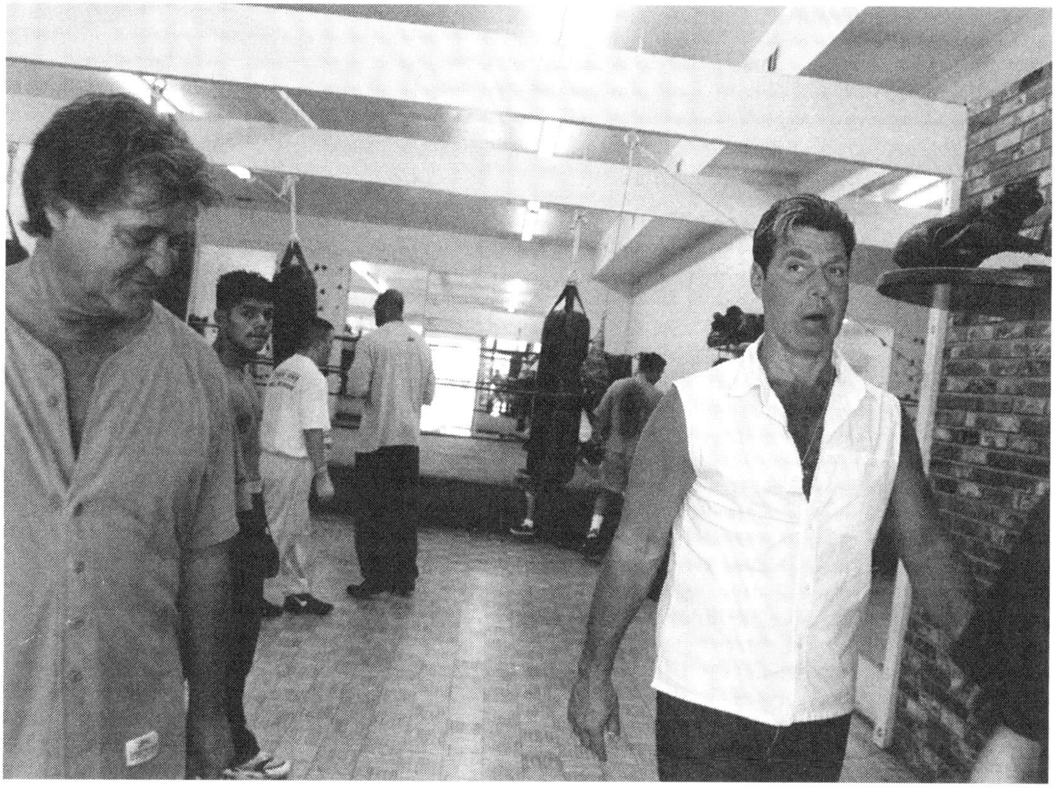

P.J. was anxious for the fight. Not many fighters get the chance to fight a great champion. P.J. was not intimidated. Although Duran was one of his heros, a win would raise P.J.s ranking.

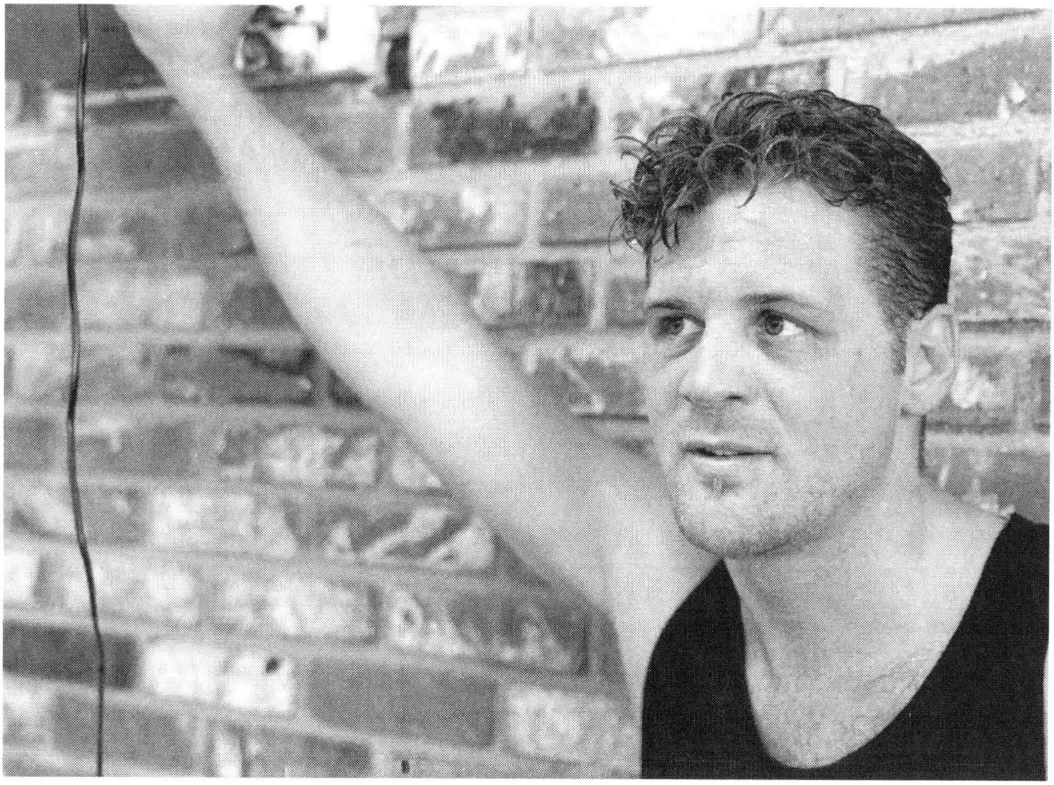

The running starts immediately. Duran was up at dawn with manager Tony.

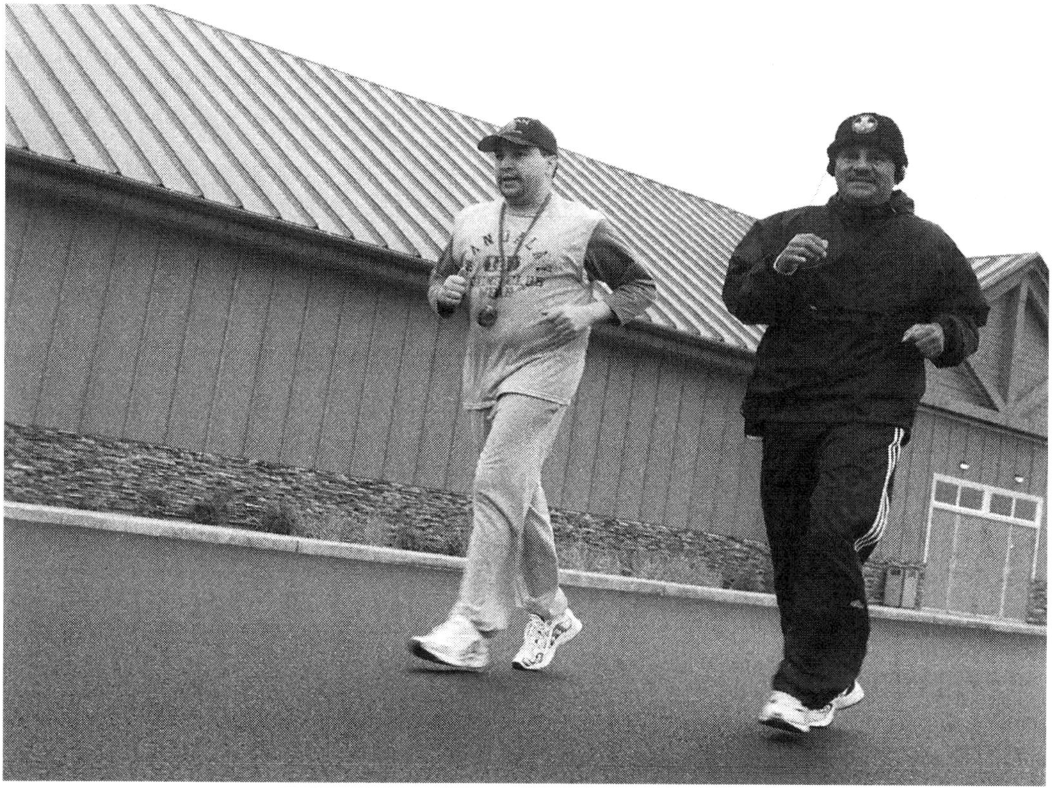

After jogging, Duran takes a nap, then has breakfast. About 1:00 he starts his workout. Here he works the speed bag, his least favorite activity.

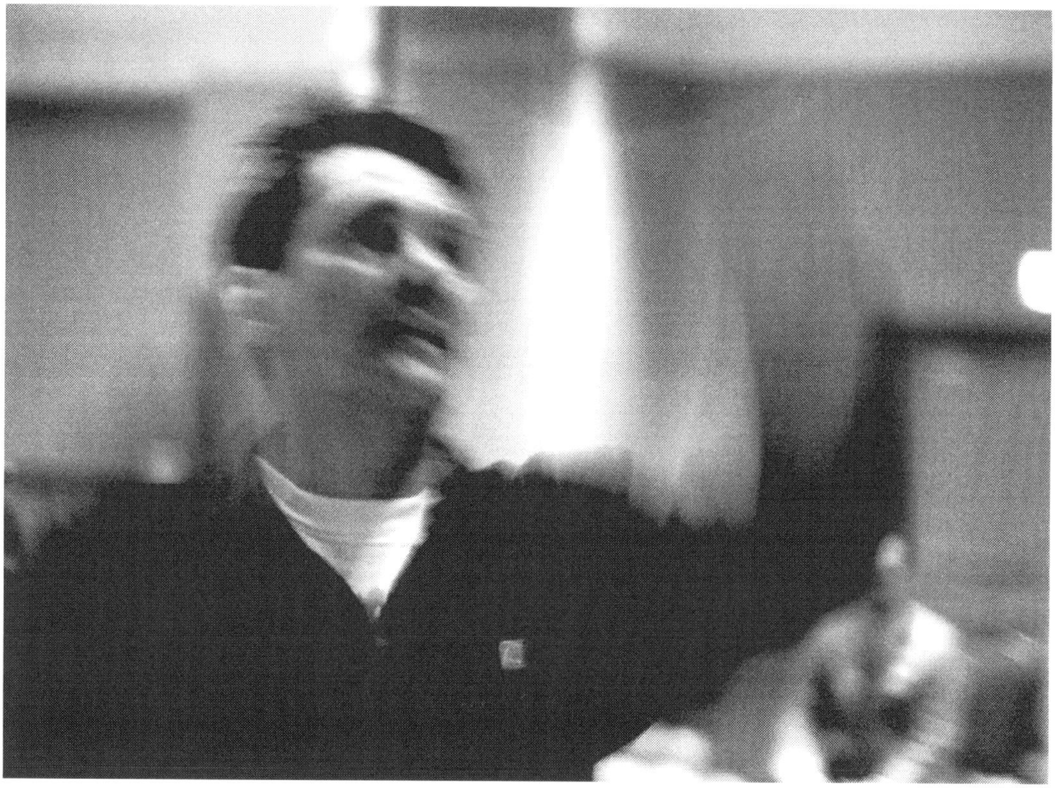

More running follows later in the day. He outjogs Tony and often laughs at him for not keeping up.

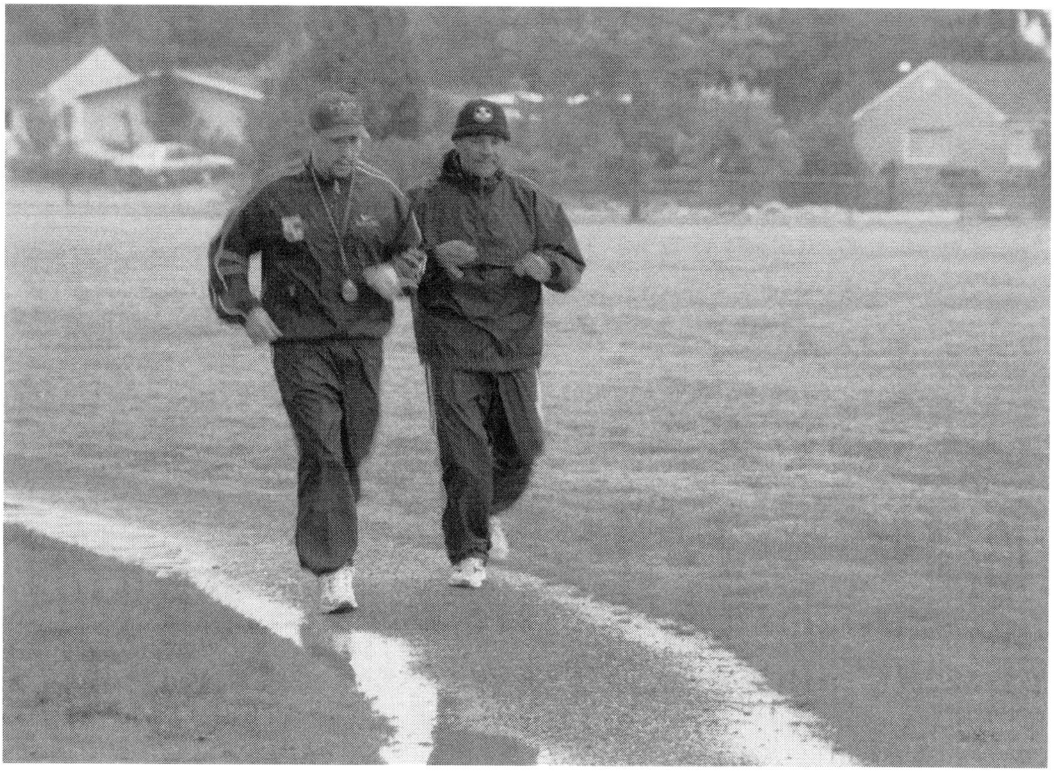

Nestor has trained Duran for many years and they are friends. He laughs easily and seldom gets upset.

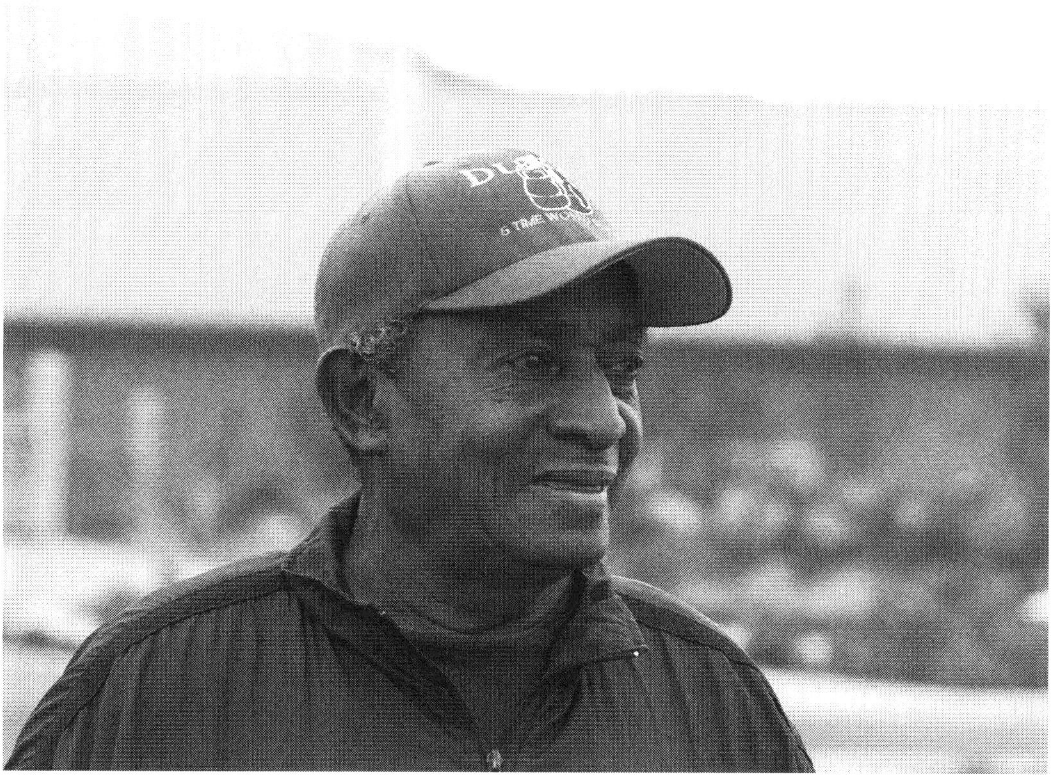

The casino offers many quiet places to run. Duran runs several miles every day and enjoys the scenic surroundings.

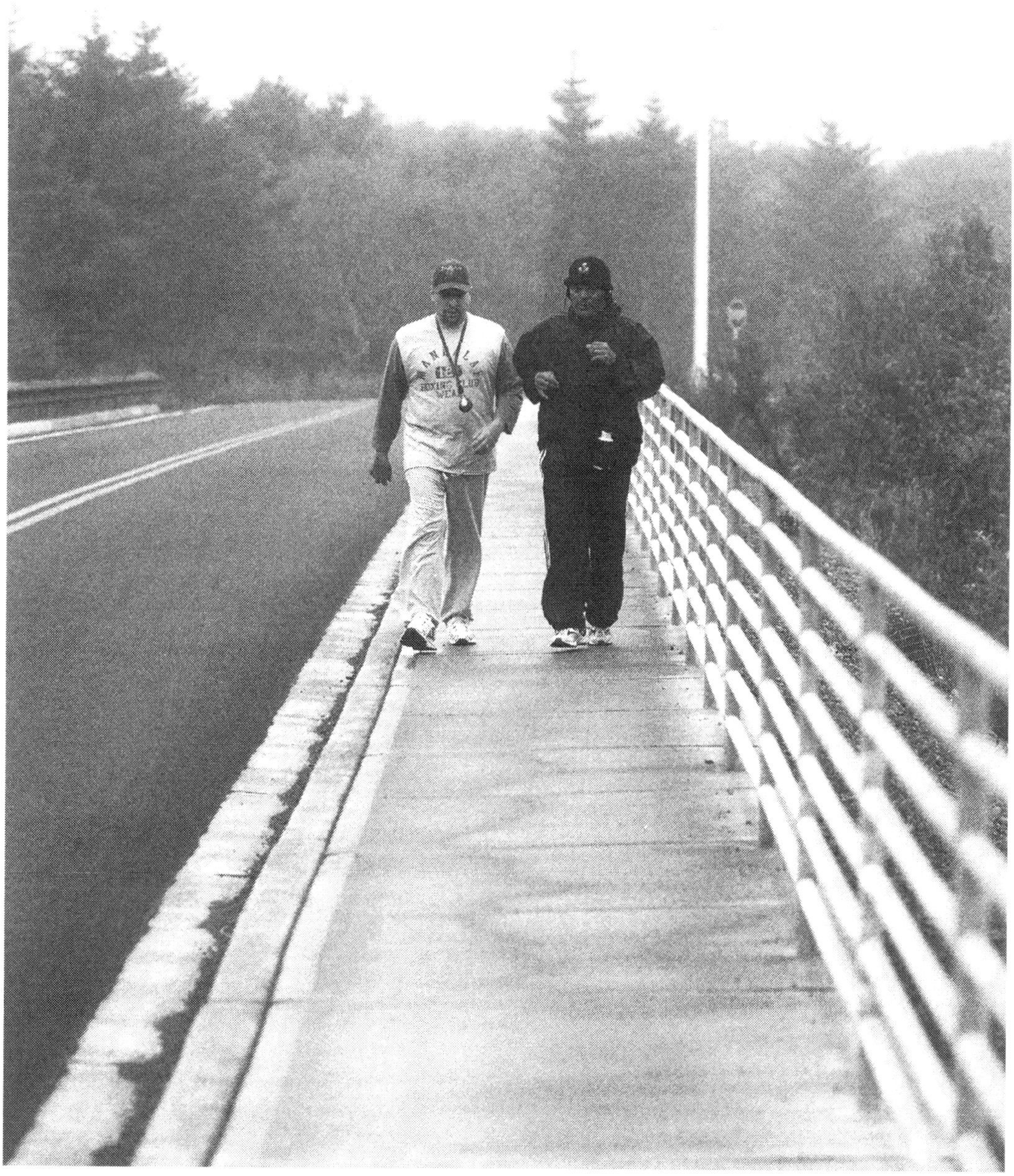

Tony and Nestor discuss the upcoming fight. Duran is 50 years old and any fight is tough at that age. His opponent, P.J. Goossen is no slouch, no set-up boxer. Goossen is young, can fight, and he is coming to win.

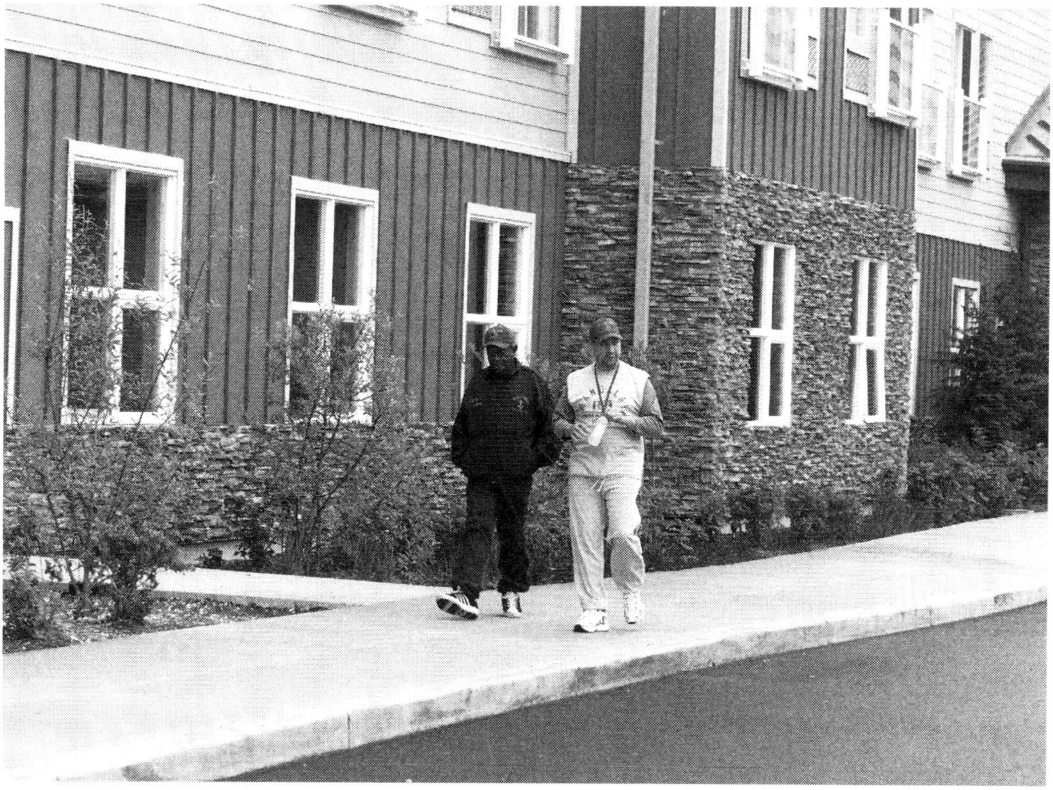

Anthony Hunter trains fighters in Tacoma, Washington. He comes along to help out and to pick up some pointers from Nestor. The two hit it off immediately.

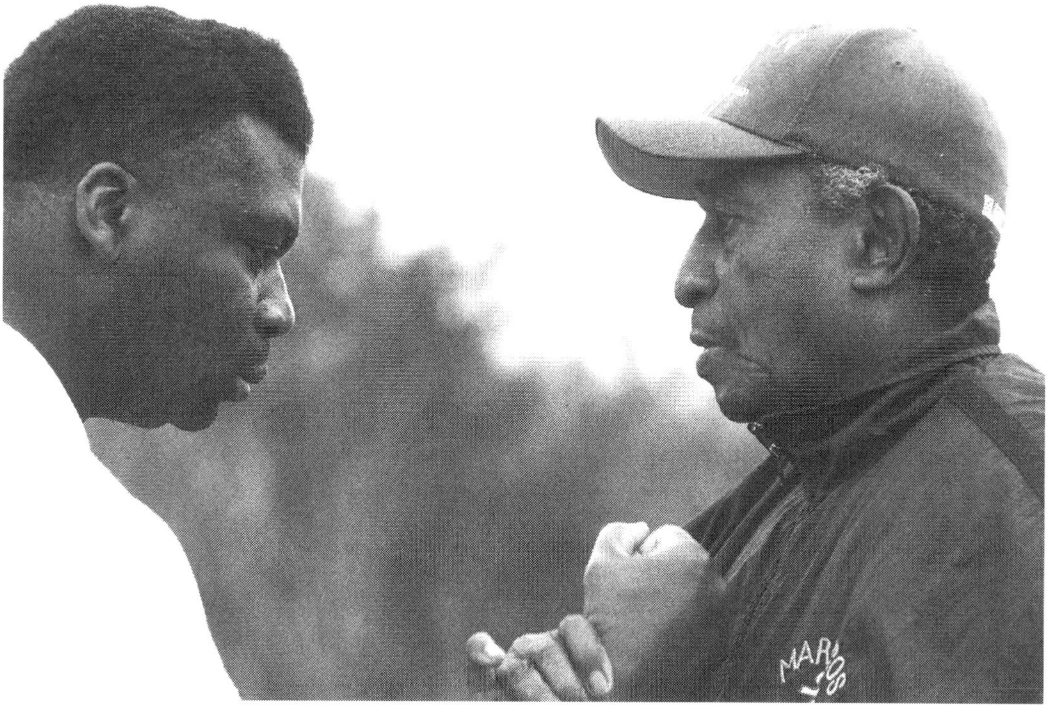

A ring is erected in a large room at the casino. Word has gotten out that Duran is training there and crowds start to gather. Duran is on a publicity tour for the fight and started training at the Lucky Eagle Casino. From Quinault he will train at the Emerald Queen before moving on to the fight at the Legends Casino in Toppinish, Washington

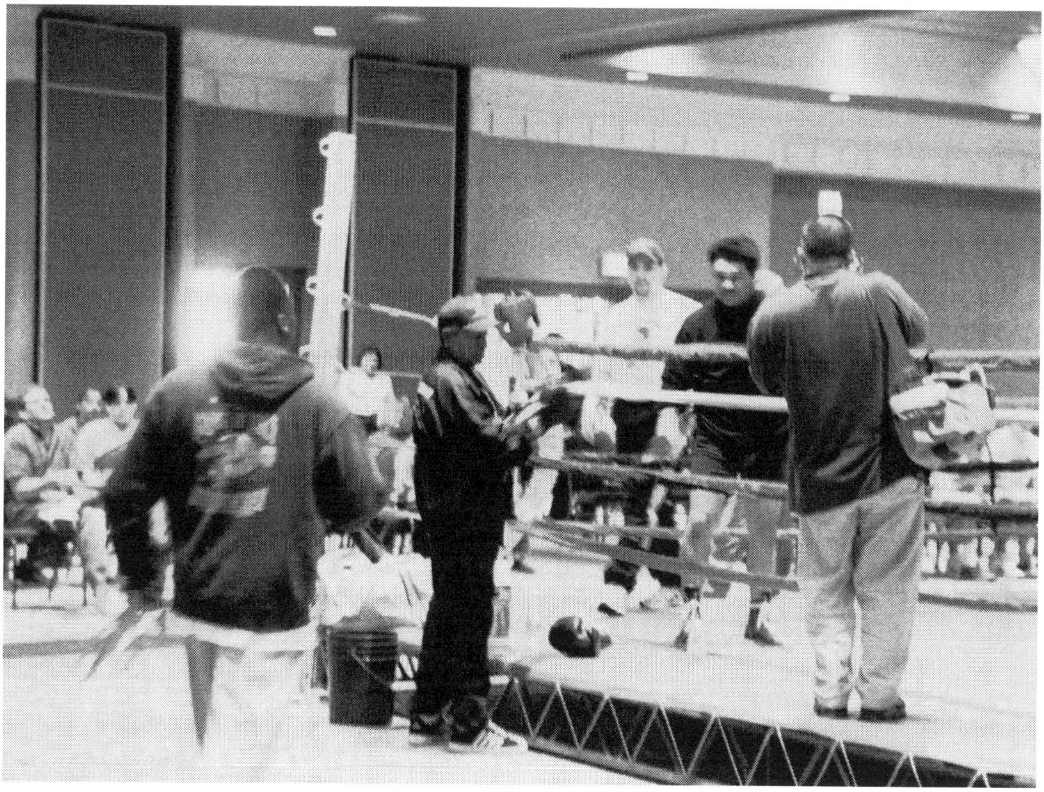

The sparring partner does not appear so Hunter steps in. He has never boxed before. Hunter gives Duran his best, but when he gets clocked with a left to the head he calls it quits. Duran does not understand the problem until he is told that Hunter has never boxed. Duran laughs and admires Hunter for his guts. He asks Hunter to join his team in training and to work the corner at the fight. Hunter is thrilled. Few people can say they have worked with a world champion.

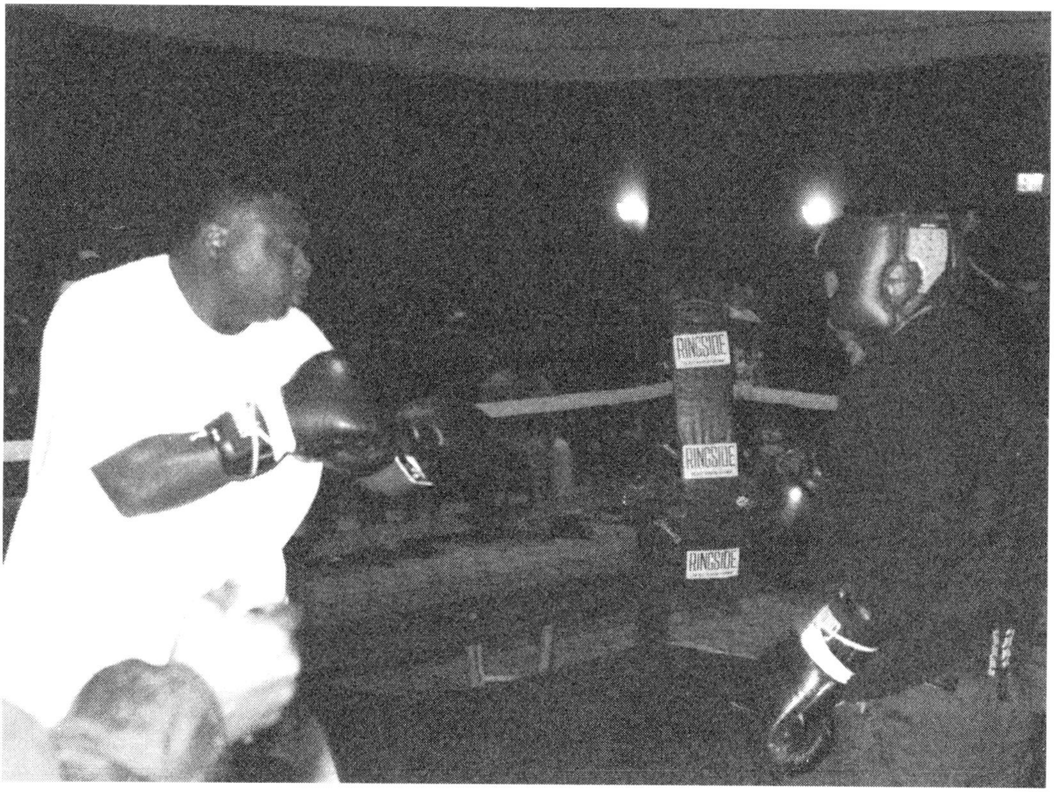
RINGSIDE
RINGSIDE
RINGSIDE

Each day the crowds get bigger. Duran is in his own world. When not training he is affable and friendly, always a smile on his face. While training he spends little time with anyone, is surly and moody and quiet. Those who know him just keep away. He is two different people.

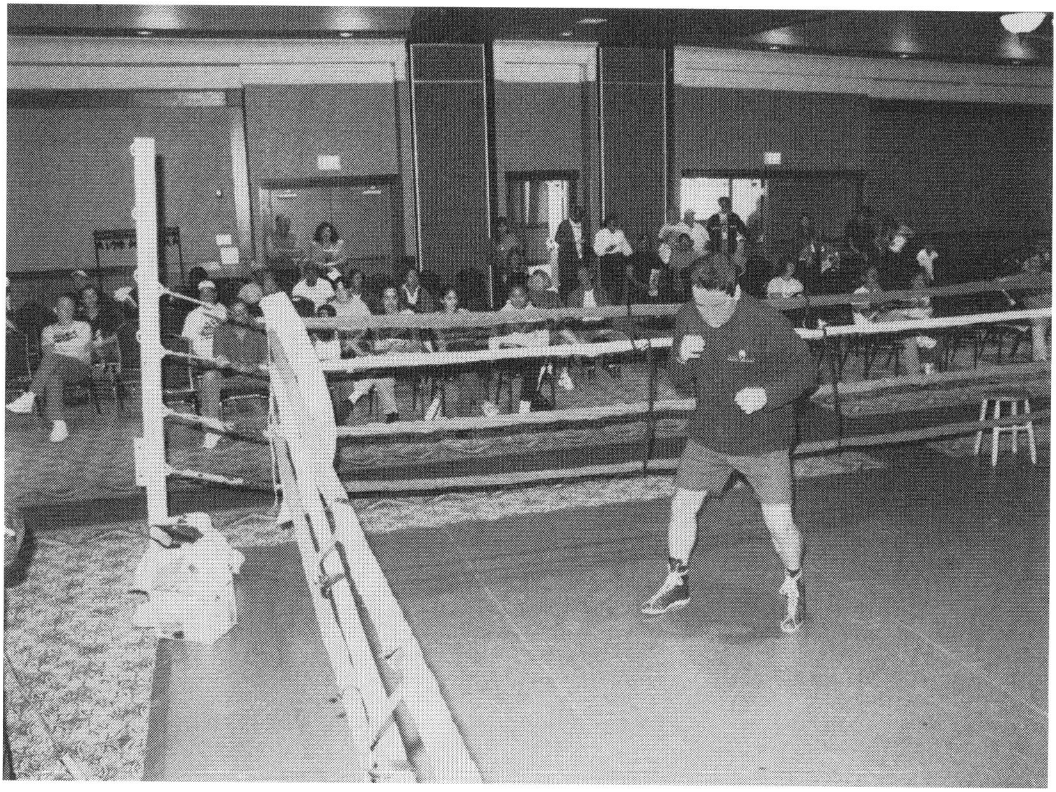

Before leaving for the Emerald Queen Casino Duran takes time to sign posters and gloves for the Casino. His little finger is starting to bother him but he says nothing, just keeps it taped to another finger.

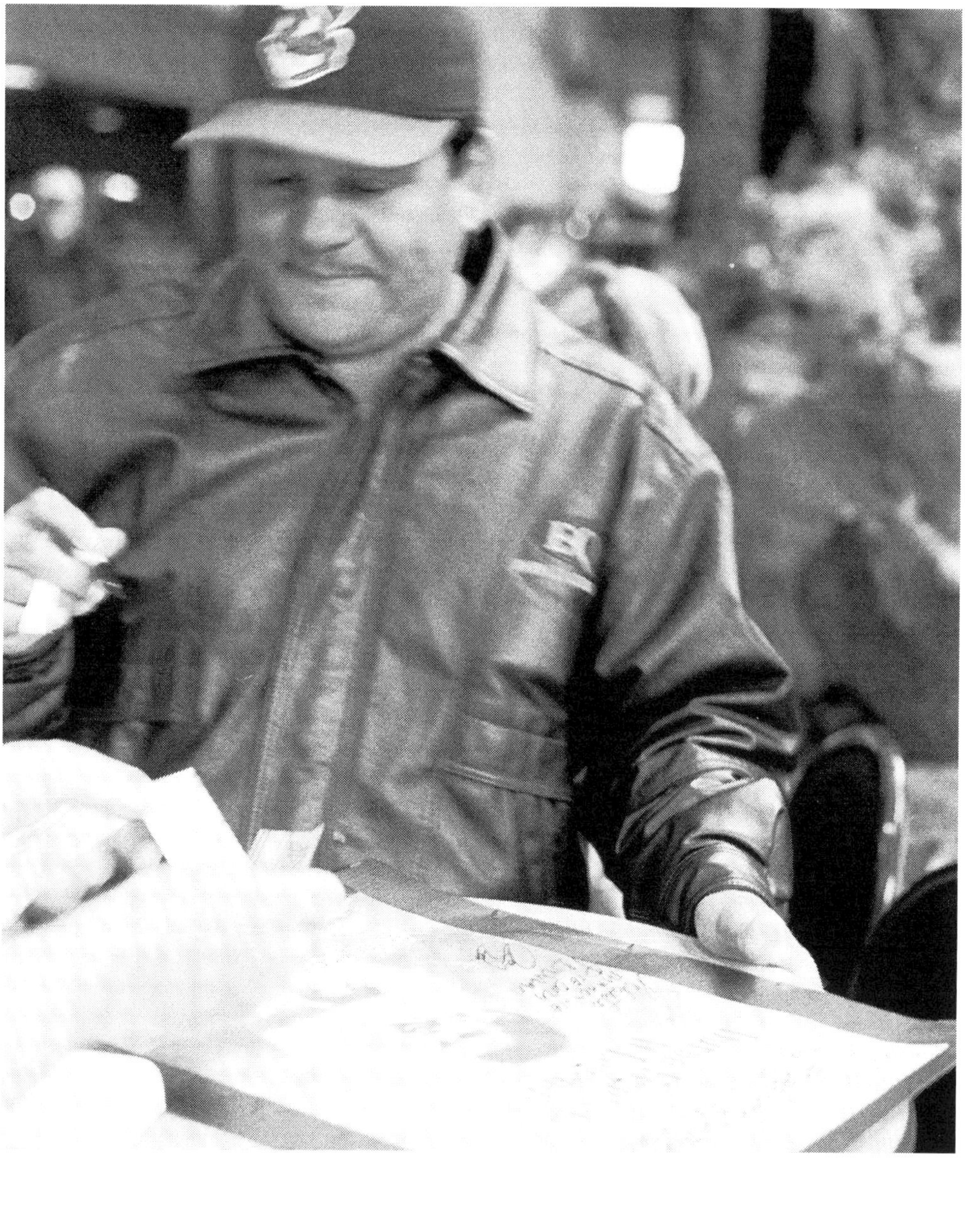

The work is starting to show. A 50 year old body is tough to keep in shape and most people simply exchange exercise for beer and chips. Not Duran. No one becomes champion by quitting.

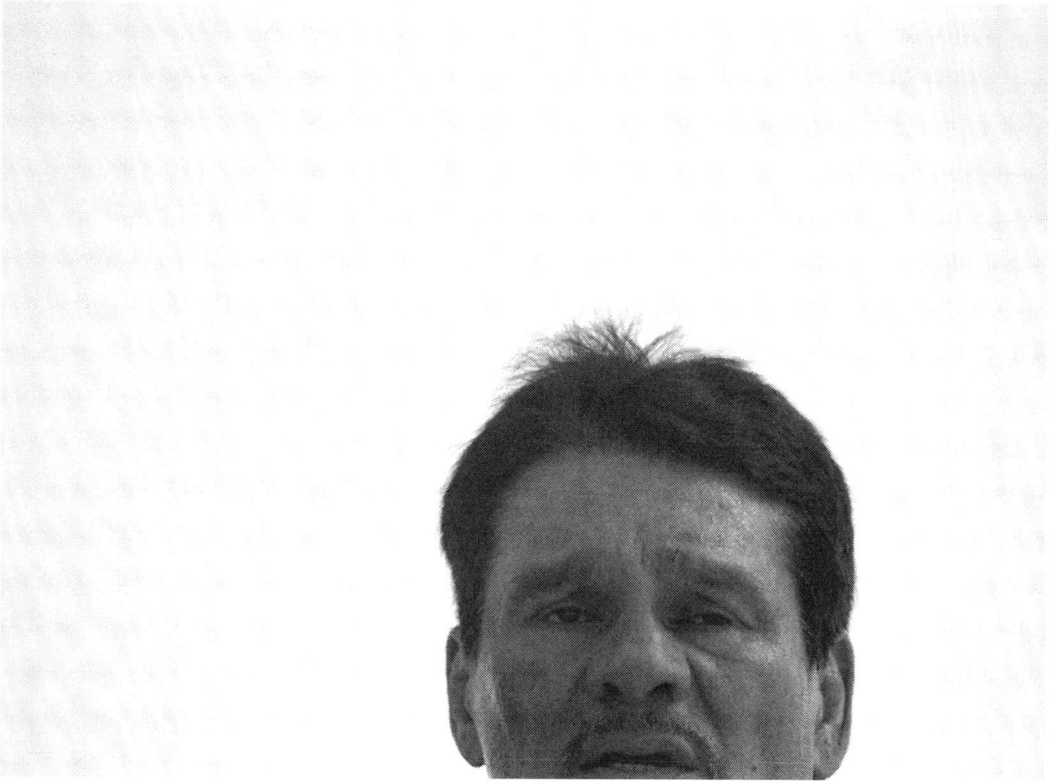

He is back in the gym and ready to go.

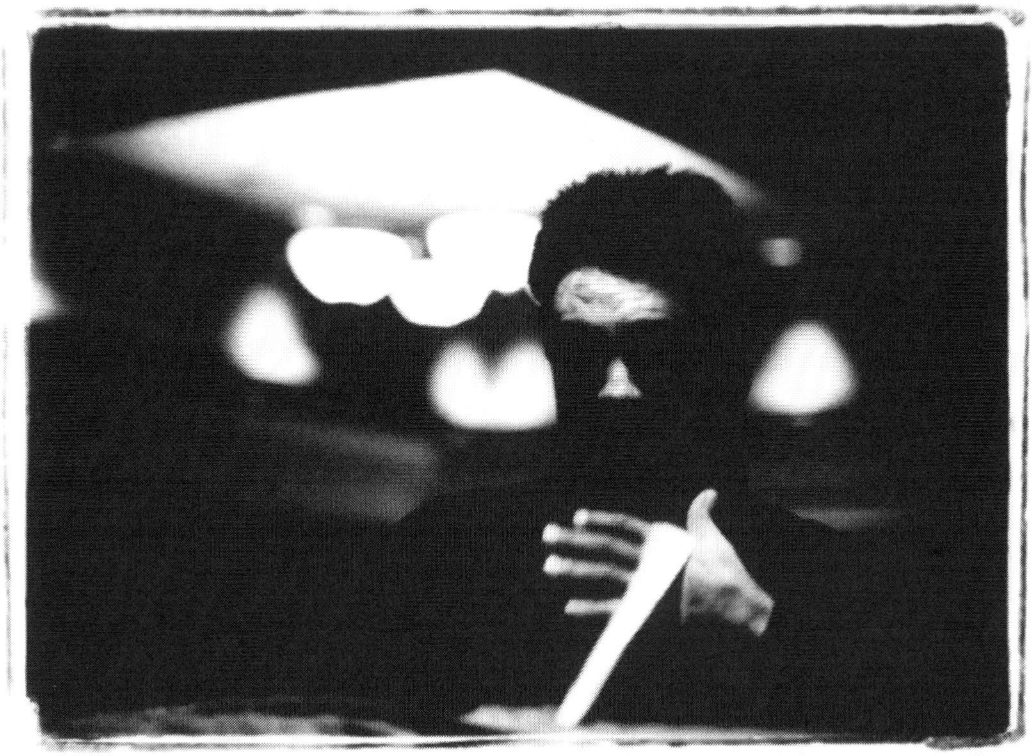

At the Emerald Queen Casino Duran picks up the pace. He has already been jogging for several hours each day, and working out two hours every afternoon. Now he adds jogging twice a day and sparring.

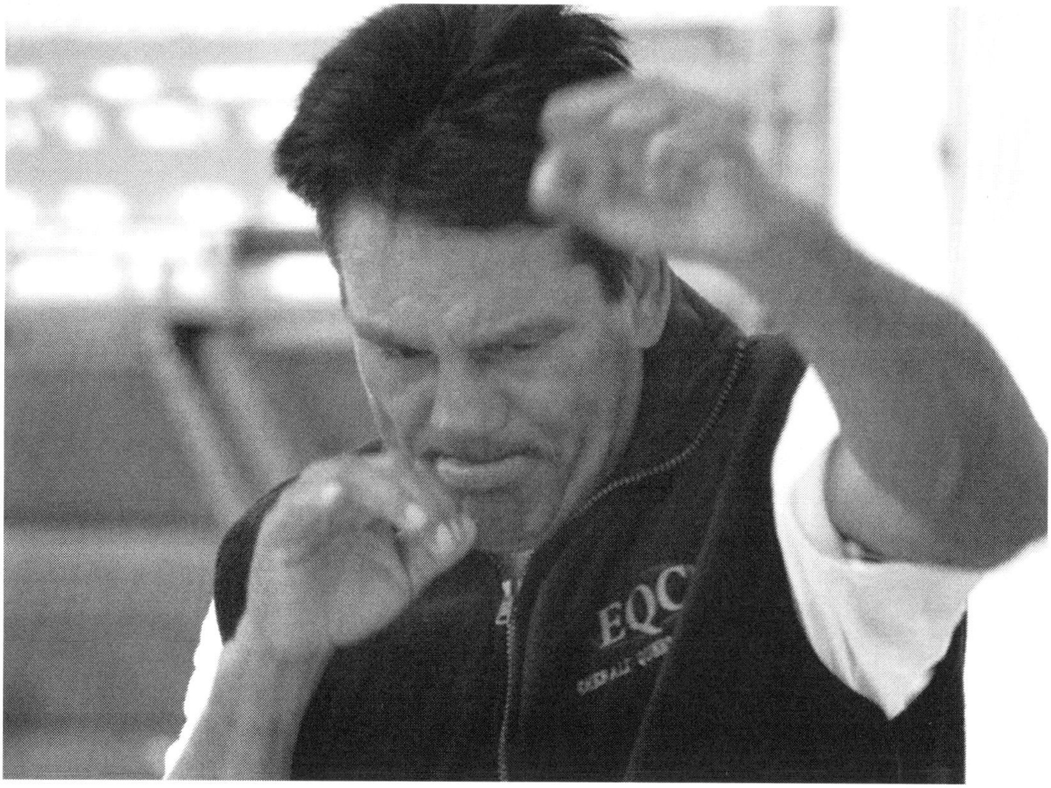

A ring is erected for the sparring.

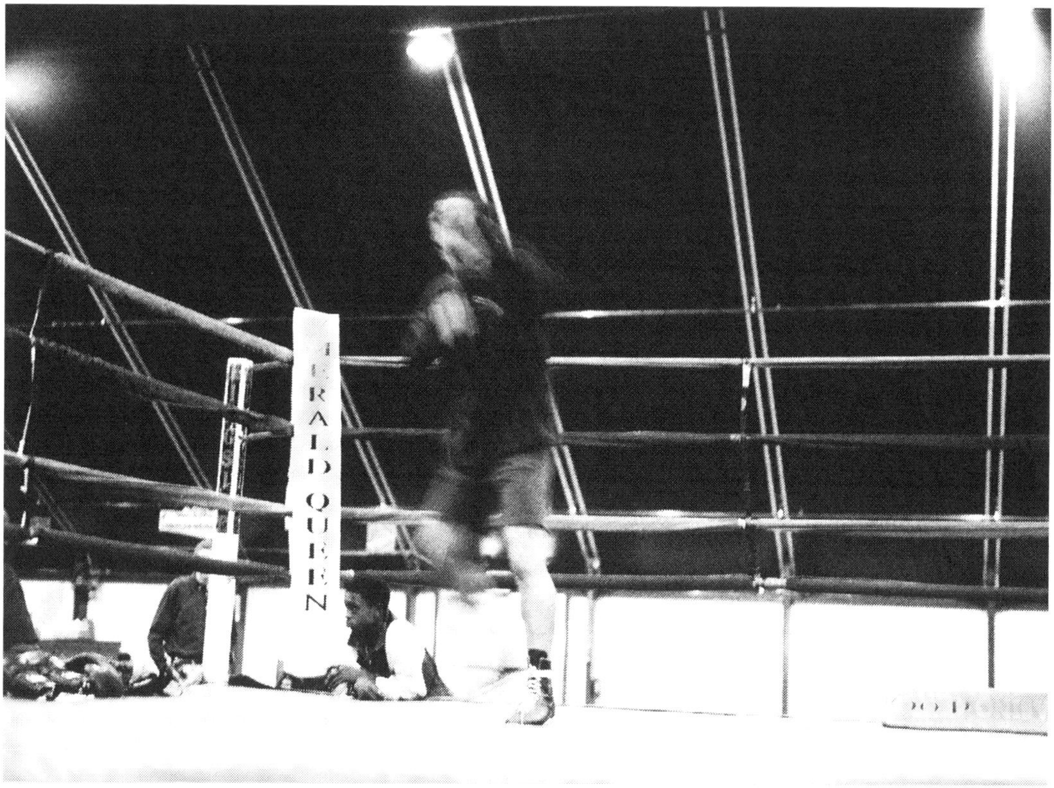
QUEEN

His favorite sparring partner is Brock Stodden. Stodden understands that sparring is not a fight, but a chance to work on various skills.

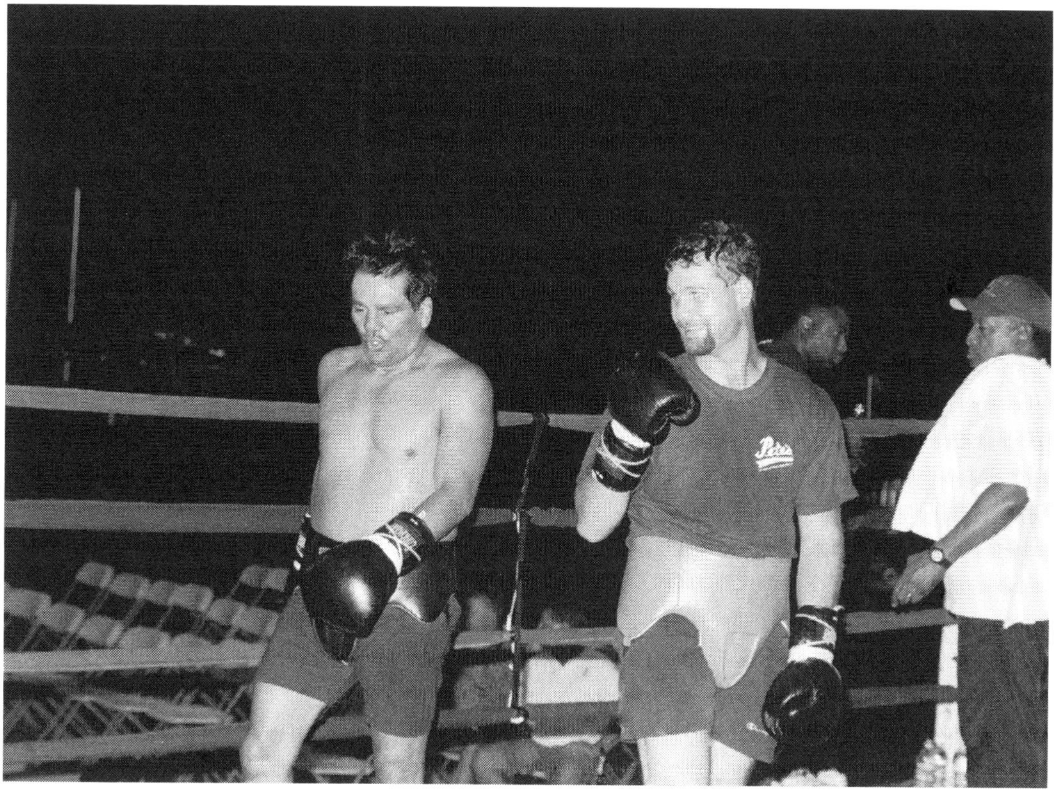

Duran finds Candy Robinson arrogant and obnoxious. Robinson wants to fight and to prove he is tough and can beat the Champion. He doesn't show up on time for sparring and says Duran can wait. He is sent packing.

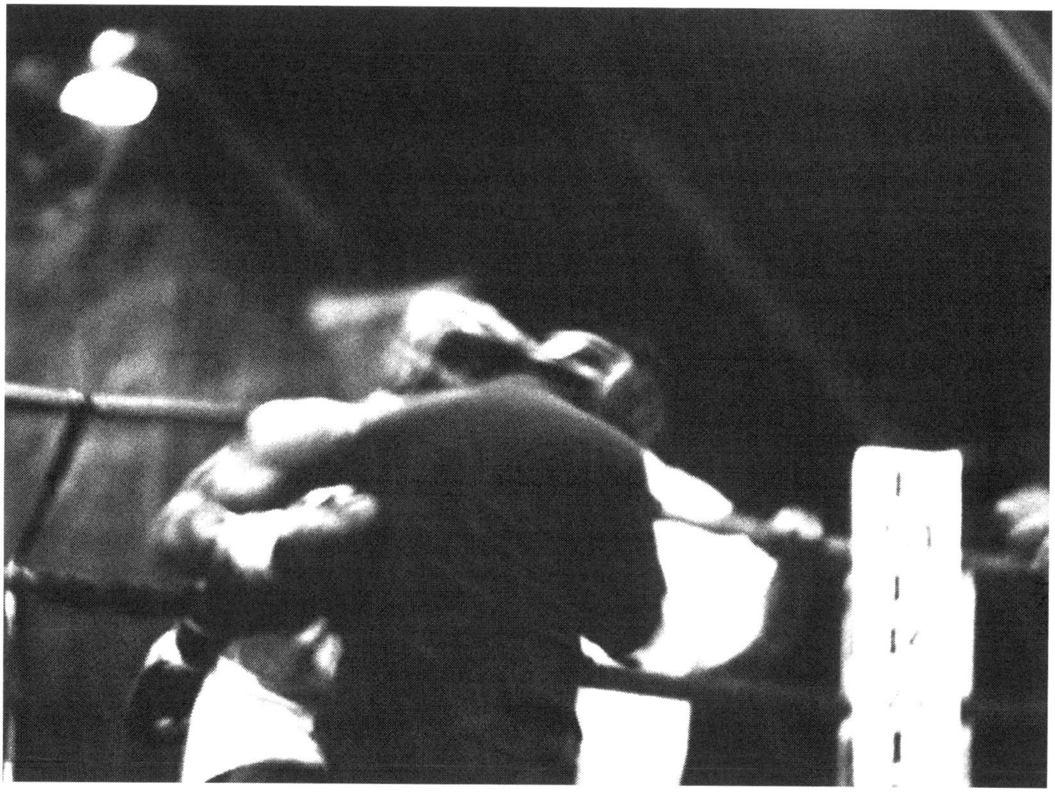

Stodden, a natural southpaw, turns righty for Duran. Stodden has excellent skills, but no chin. His career is constantly derailed because of it.

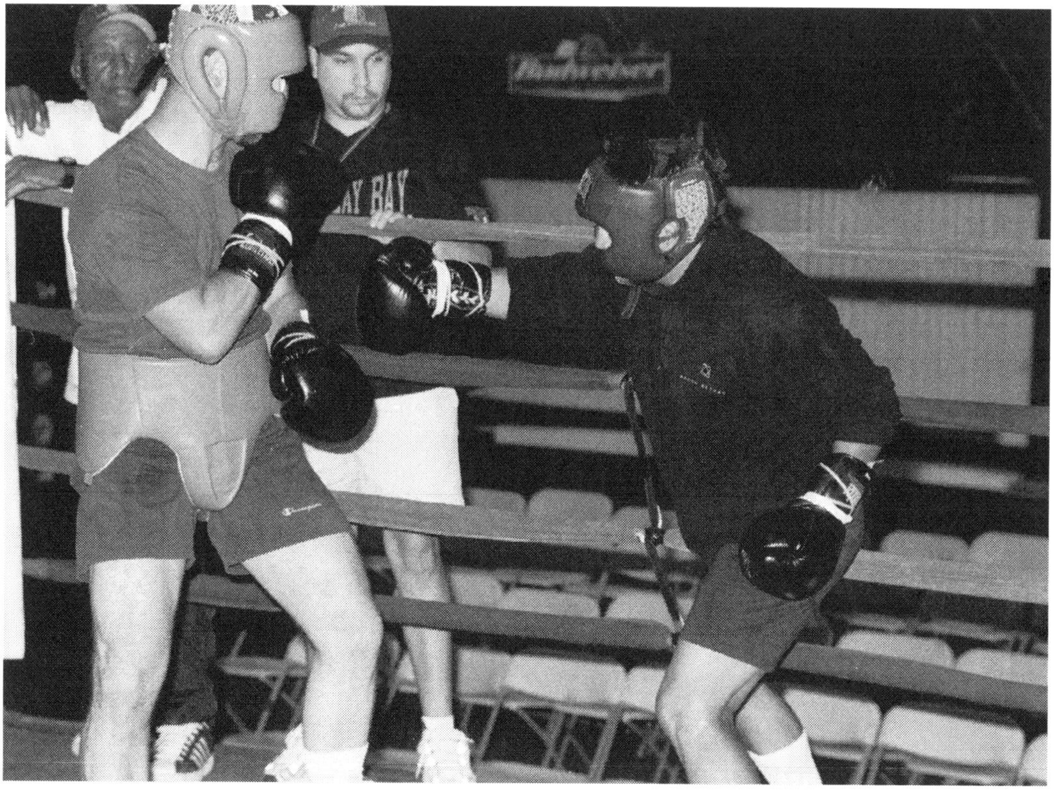

After throwing a hard right, Duran feels a sudden sharp pain his little finger.

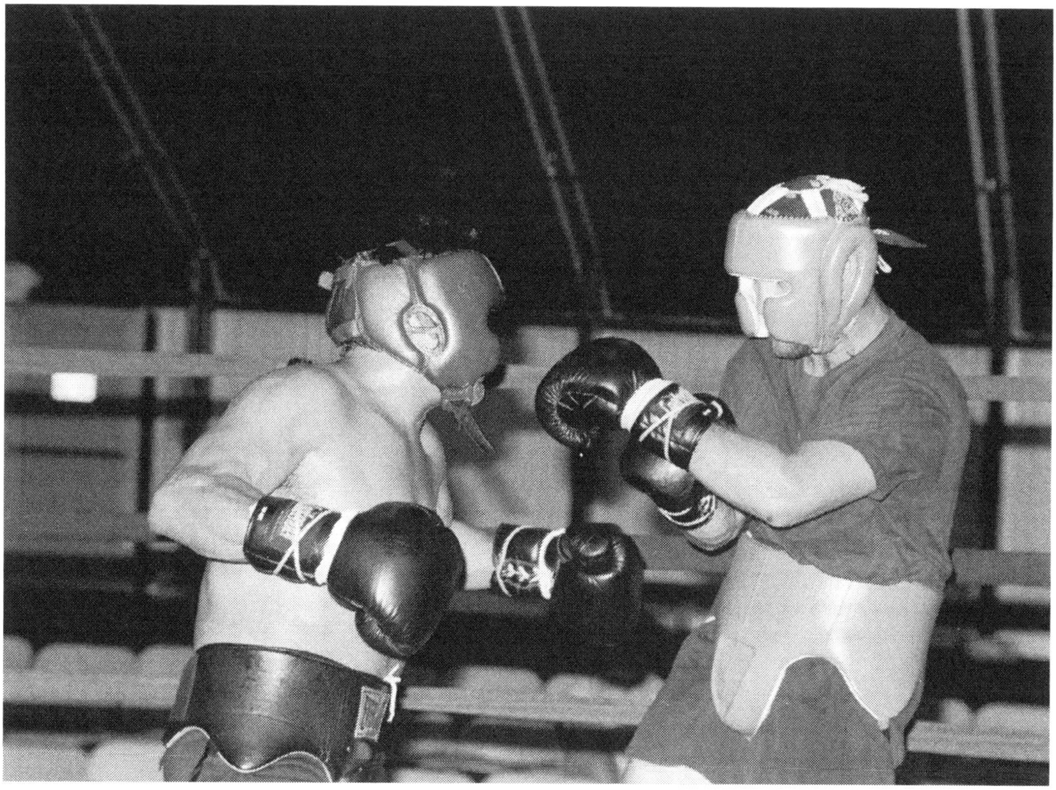

A visit to the doctor reveals the worst. Duran has fractured his finger, a long hairline break running the length of the bone. He will not let the doctor put it in a cast.

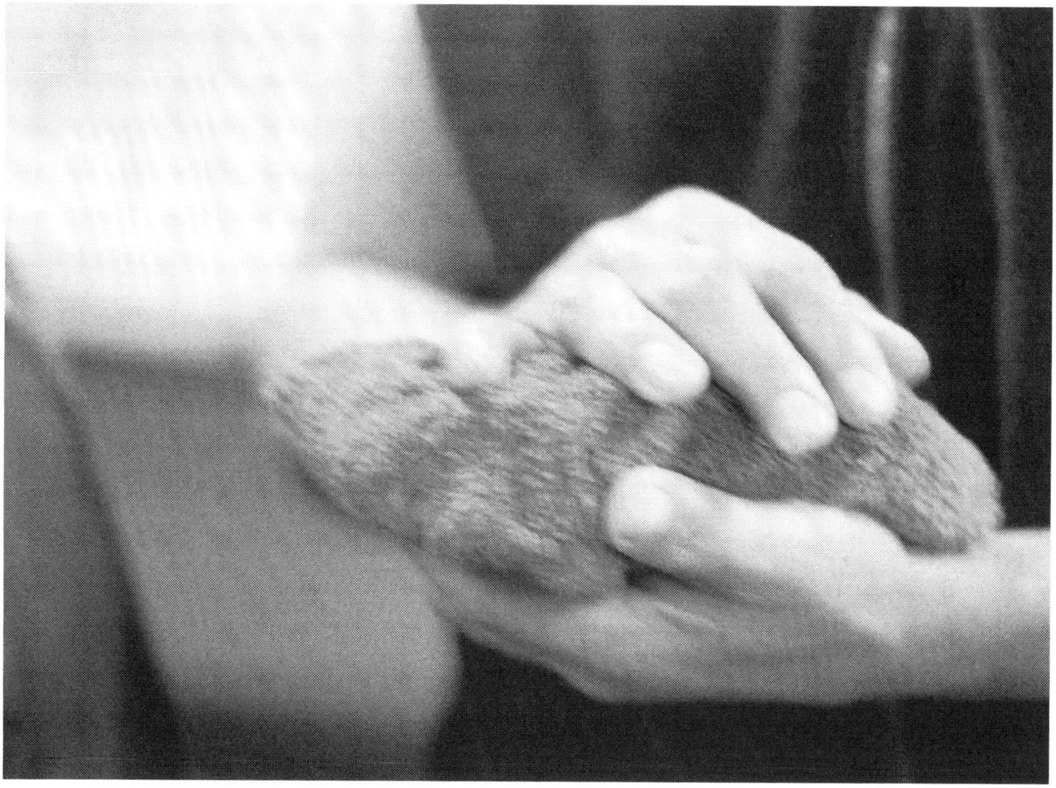

Duran discusses the problem with Tony. Any other fighter would have backed out of the bout. Not Duran. Since the break is not complete he decides to continue, keep the finger taped, and be very careful with it.

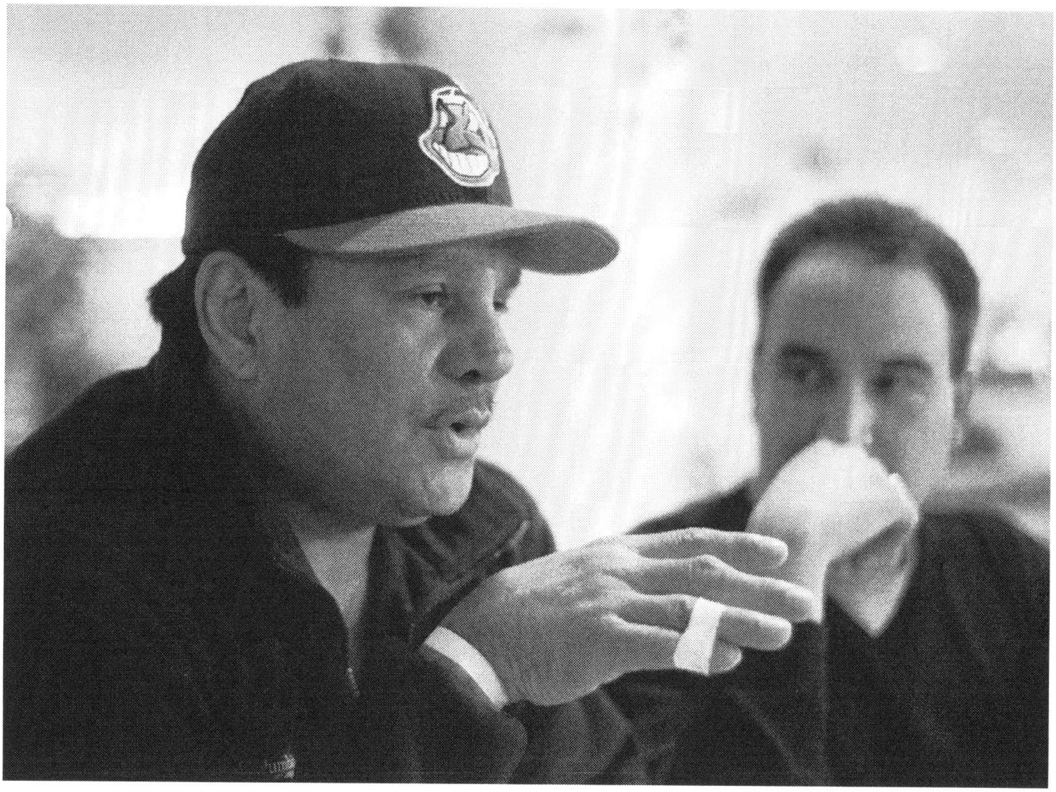

Duran's next stop is Yakama. The fight will take place nearby in Toppinish. Eastern Washington is very dry so the ring is erected outside to accommodate the large crowd.

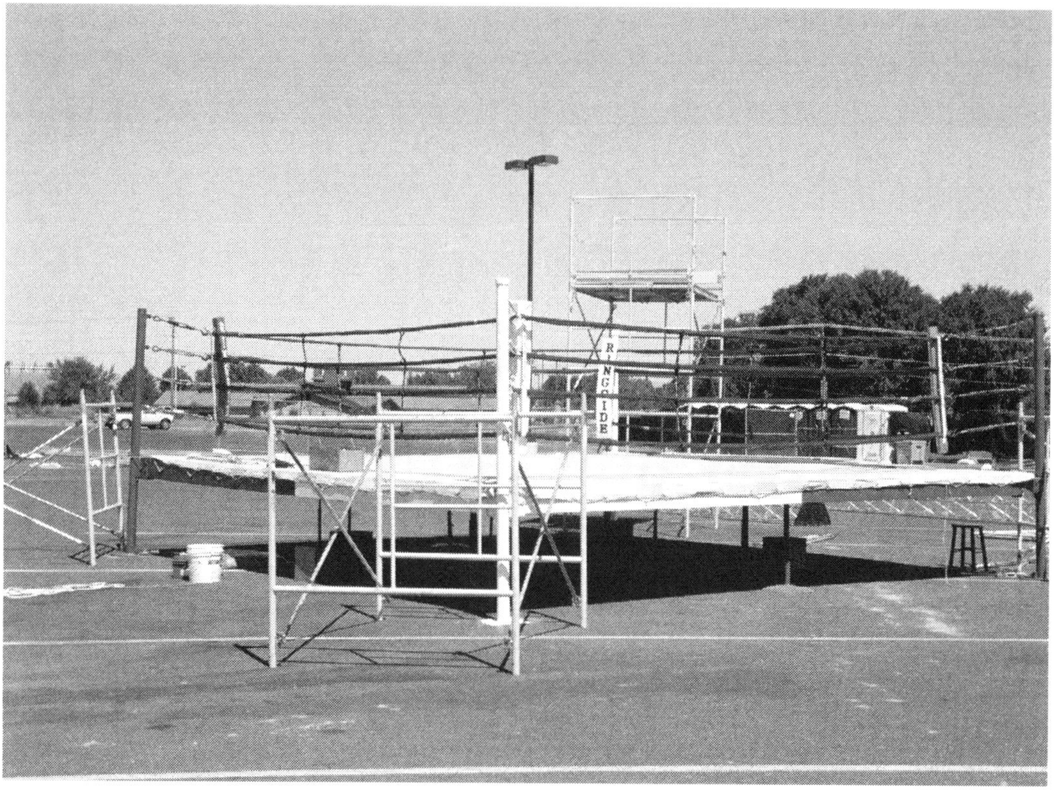
RINGSIDE

I seldom attempt to intrude in photos. People often ask why I don't have my picture taken with various personalities. I explain that because I took the picture I am in every shot. Sometimes I try and slide in a shot without notice. This is a shot of me with Duran taken in a mirror.

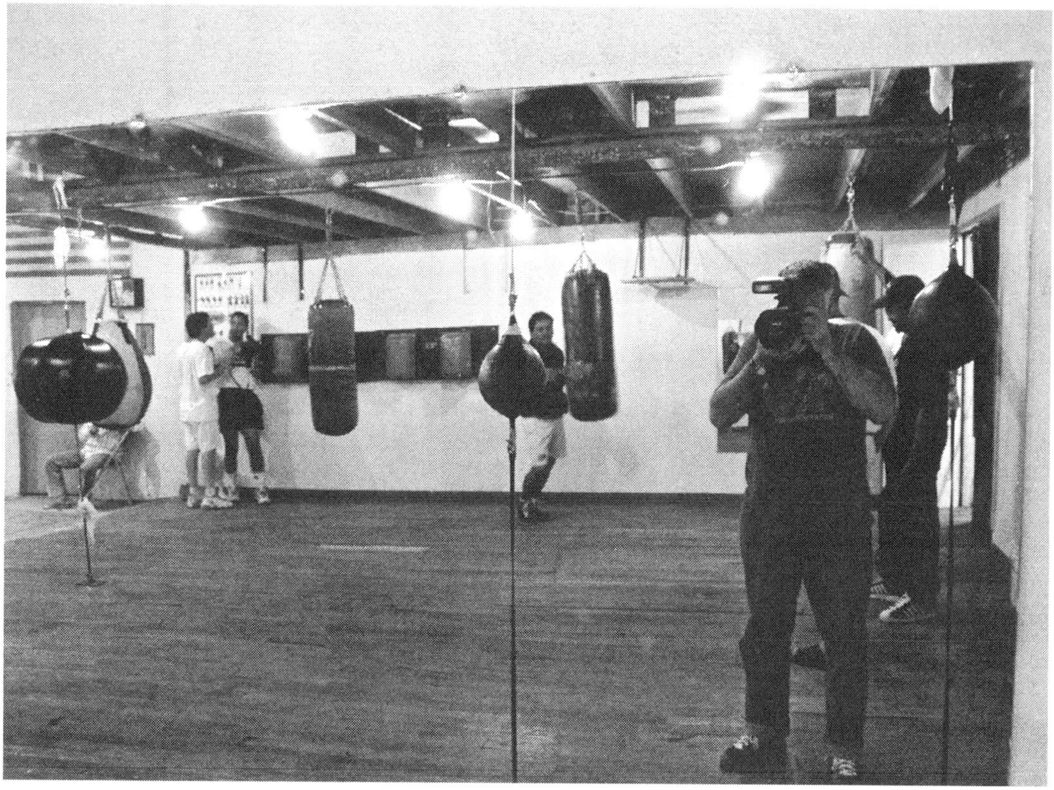

Nothing says boxing like the word monotonous. Every day the same old routine: run, eat, nap, workout, eat, run again, more sleep.

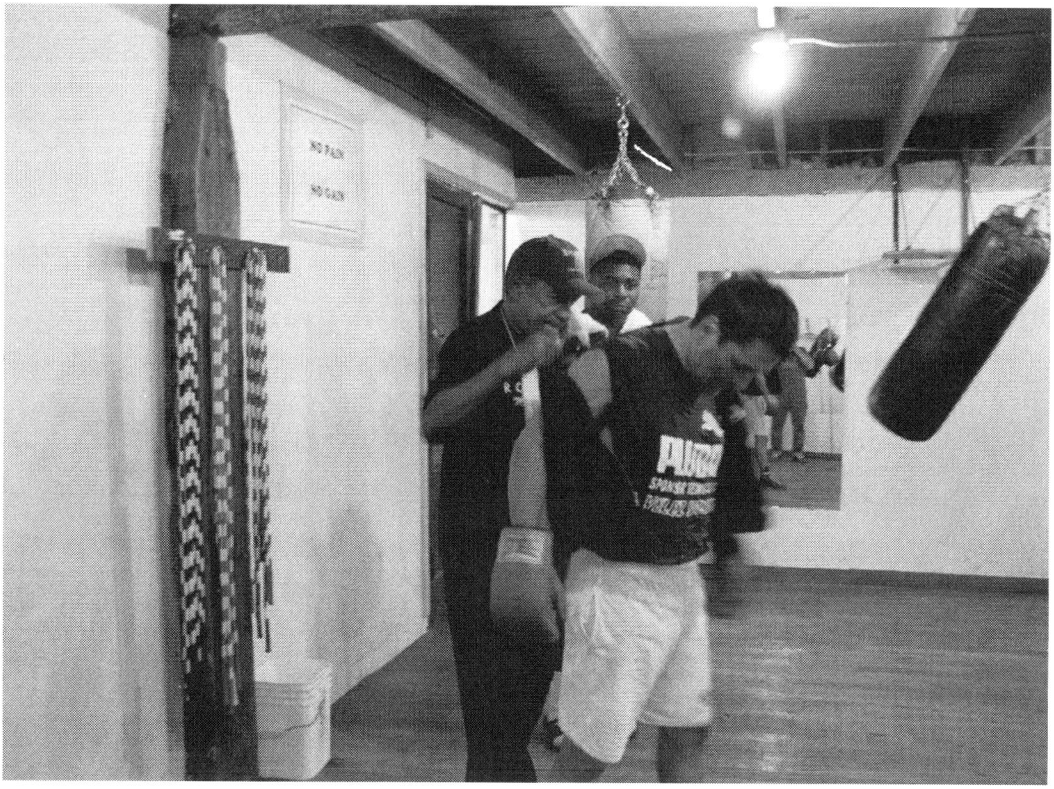

Duran is comfortable in the local gym. He does not like anything elegant.

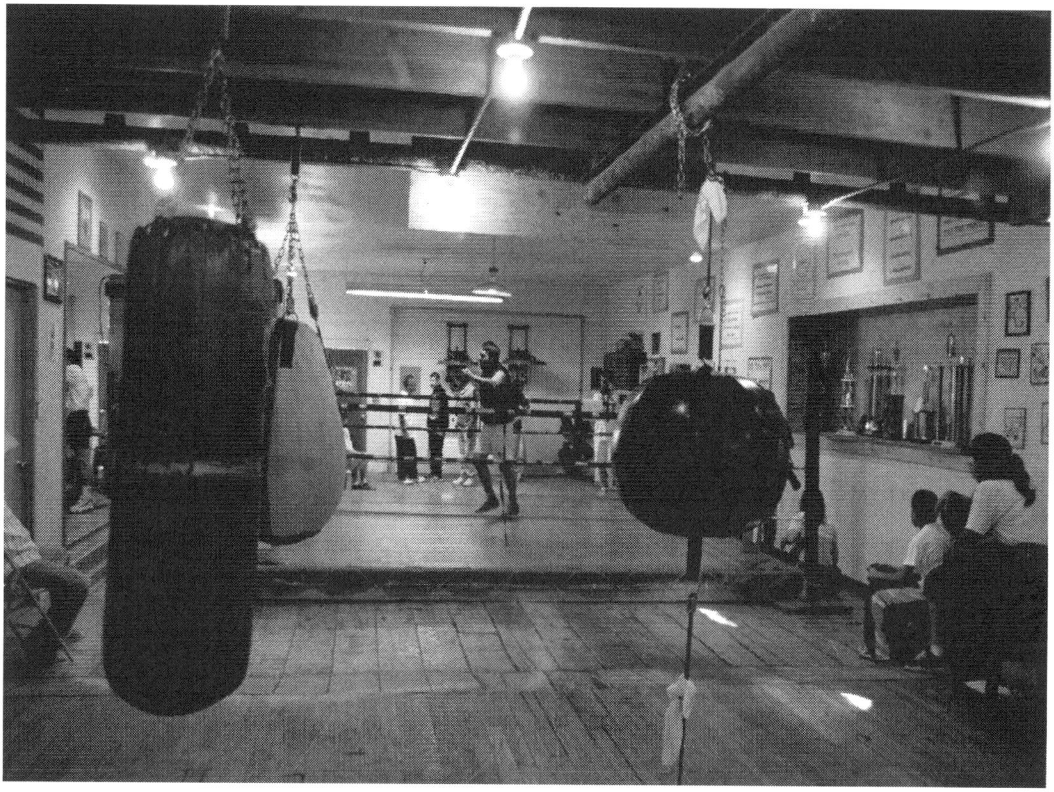

Again the word gets out and spectators and the press start to gather in the gym.

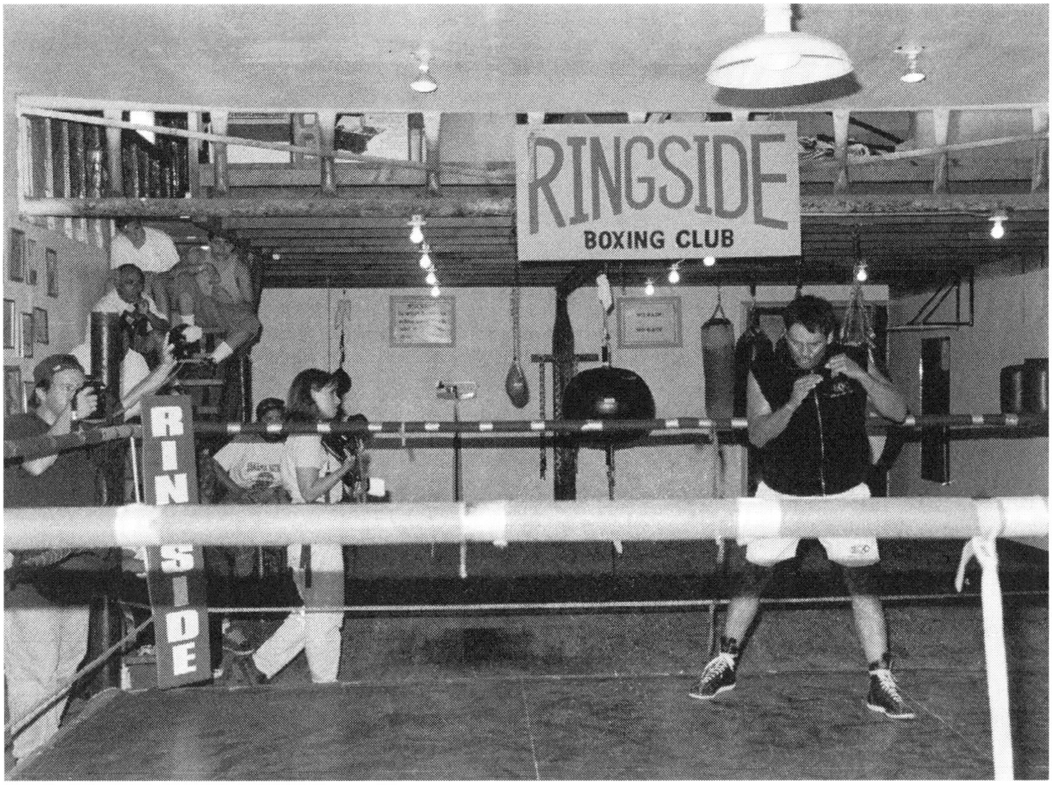
RINGSIDE
BOXING CLUB
RINGSIDE

All sparring is stopped. Duran must protect his finger and he does not want to take a chance with an accidental cut.

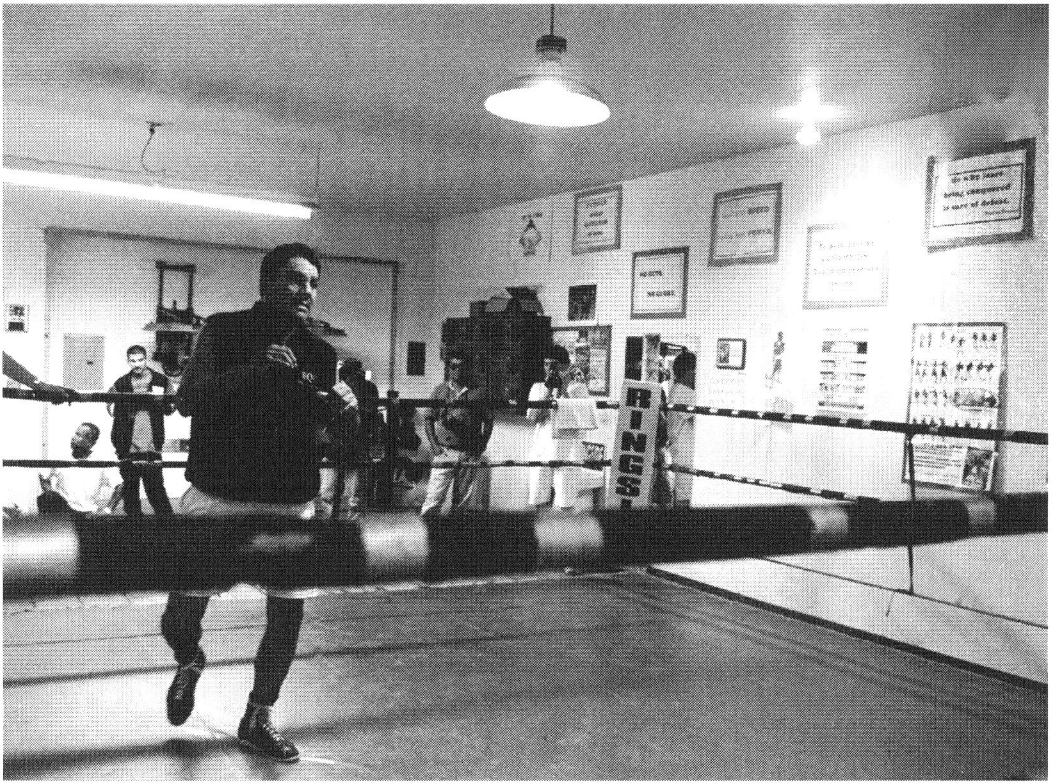
RINGS

Duran loves the heavy bag. If left alone he would work on it the entire time. Nestor must move him to the speed bag and shadow boxing.

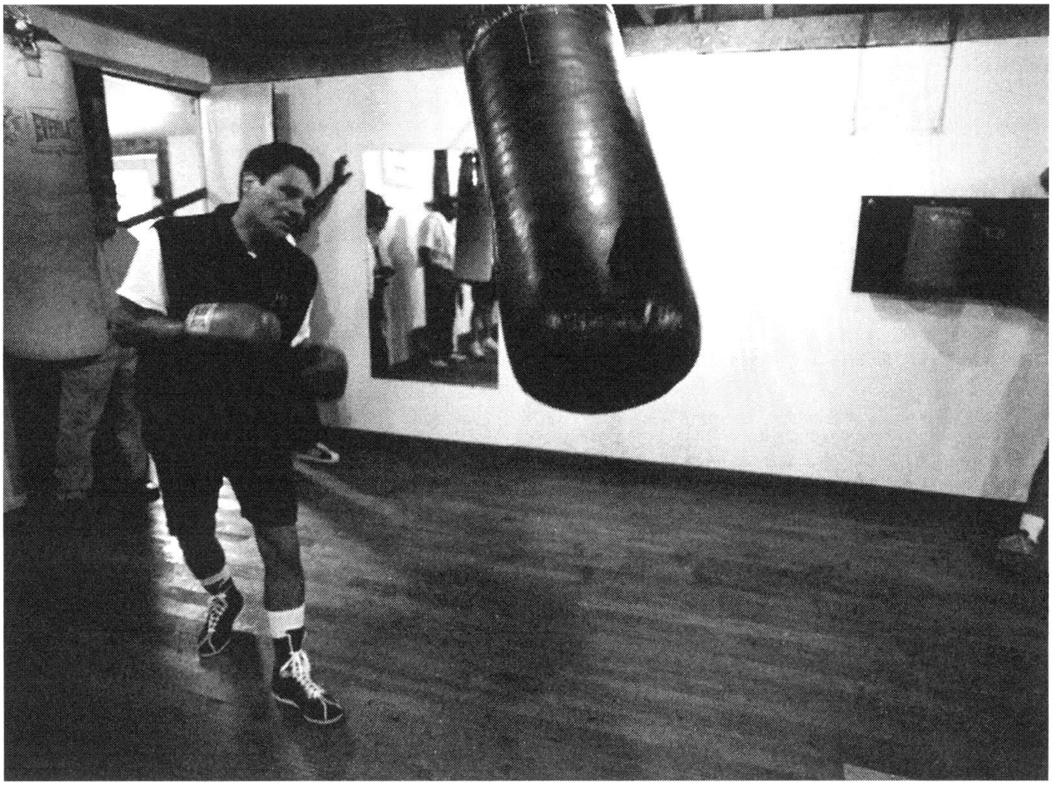

During the weeks of training Duran takes only one break. His finger is hurting a great deal so he decides to take the day off and visit Seattle.

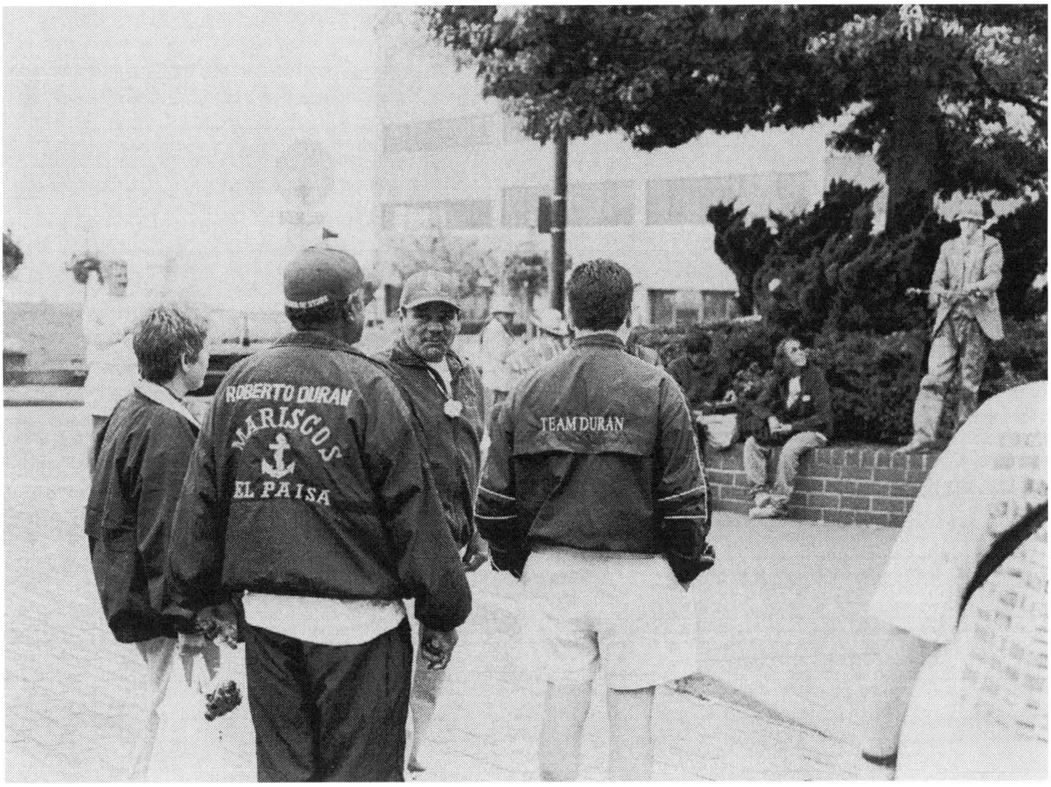

ROBERTO DURAN
MARISCOS
EL PAISA
TEAM DURAN

Although still surly and quiet, he seems to enjoy himself but people soon discover him and the crowd starts to grow. Celebrities can never have a day in public and be left alone.

Actually
worn by
WORLD'S
TALLEST
MAN
ROBERT WADLOW
(1918-1940)
actual
size

The one day vacation is far too short. The following morning he is back in the gym.

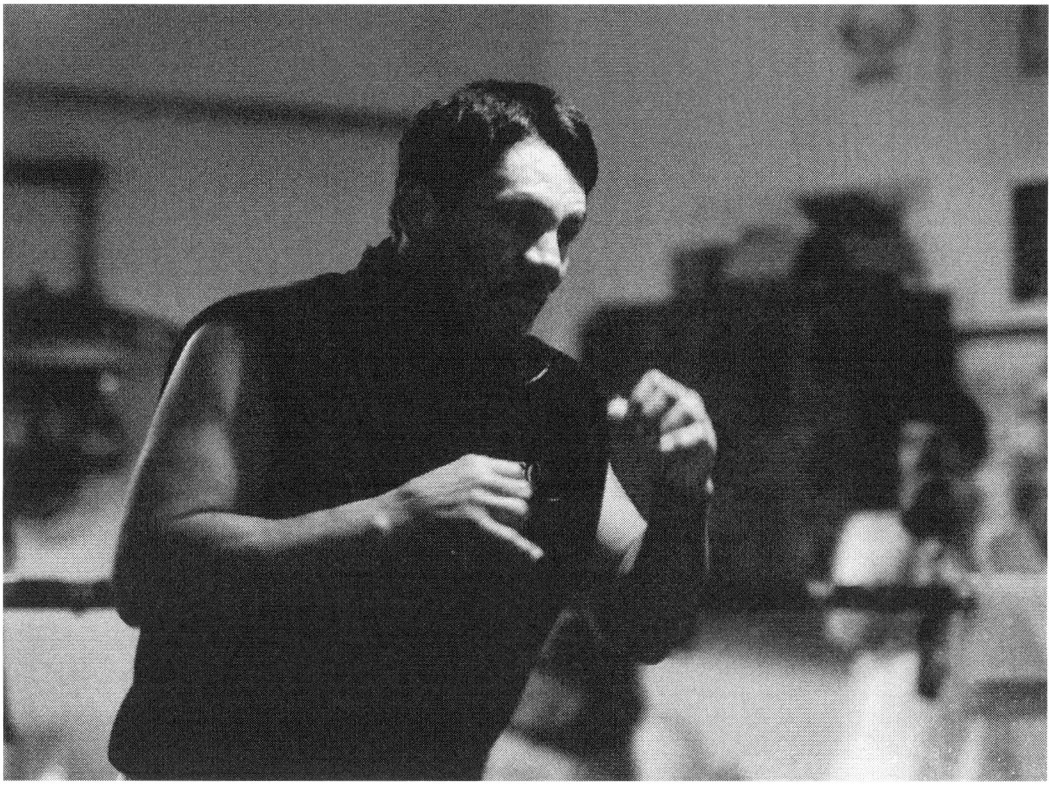

The finger is greased and wrapped very carefully before each workout.

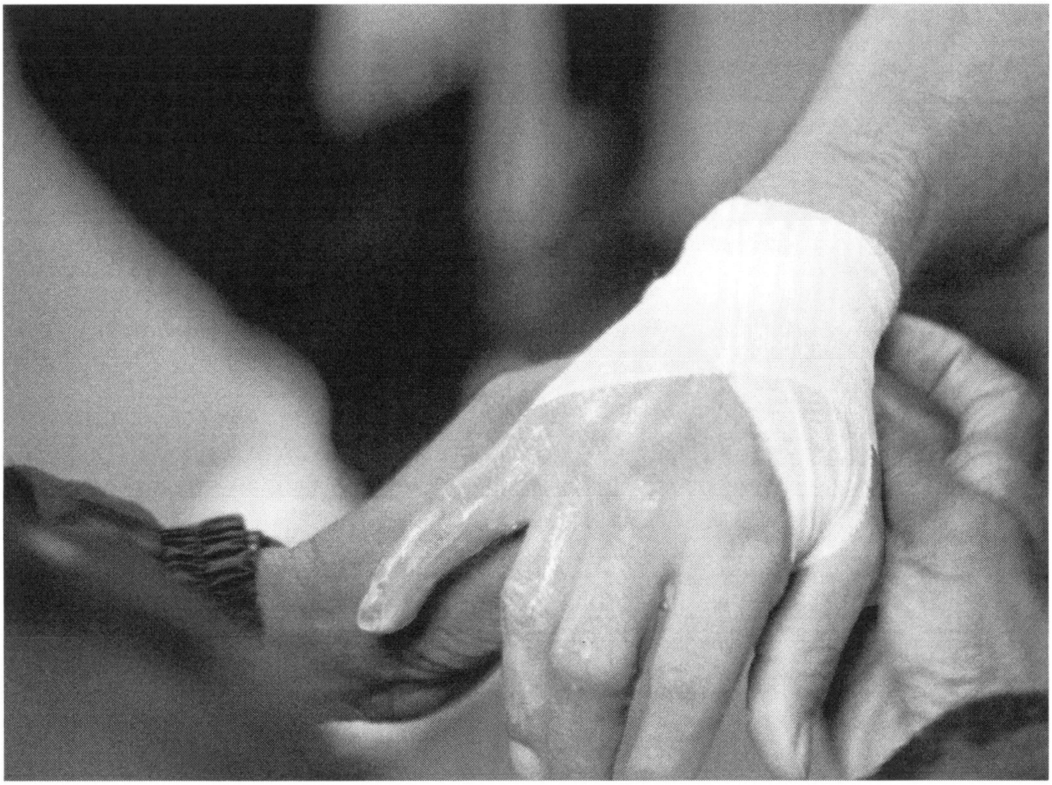

Determination shows on his face.

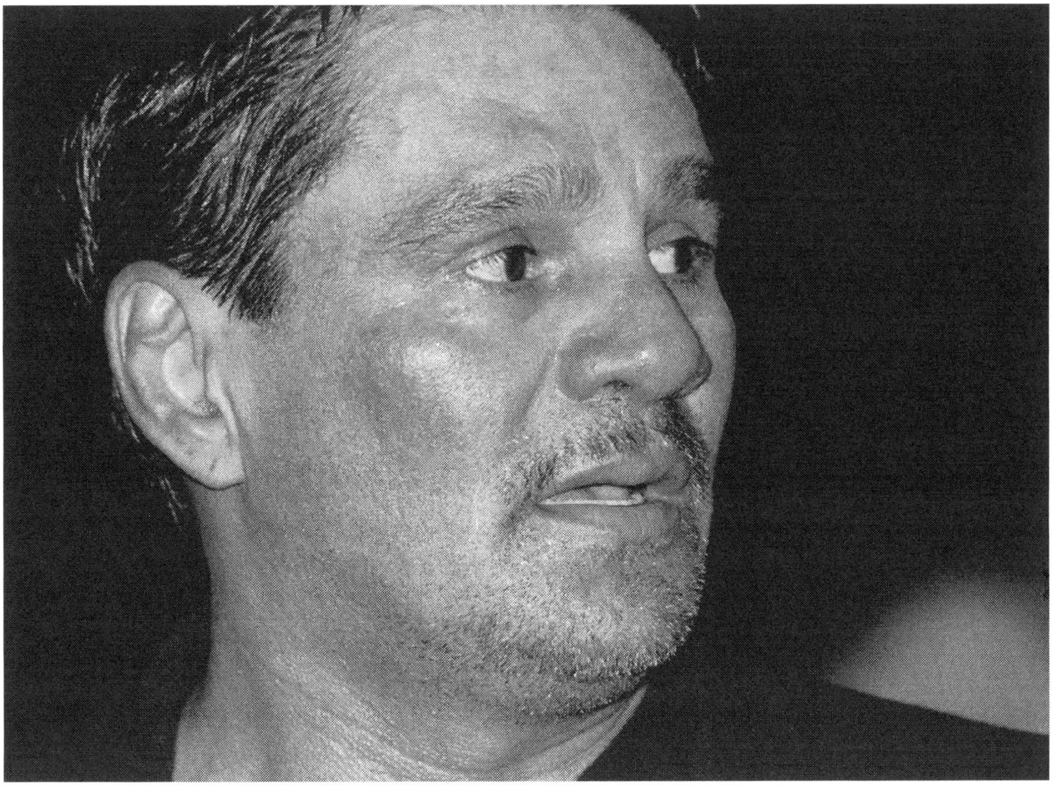

His pot belly starts to leave and he smiles again. Training is going well.

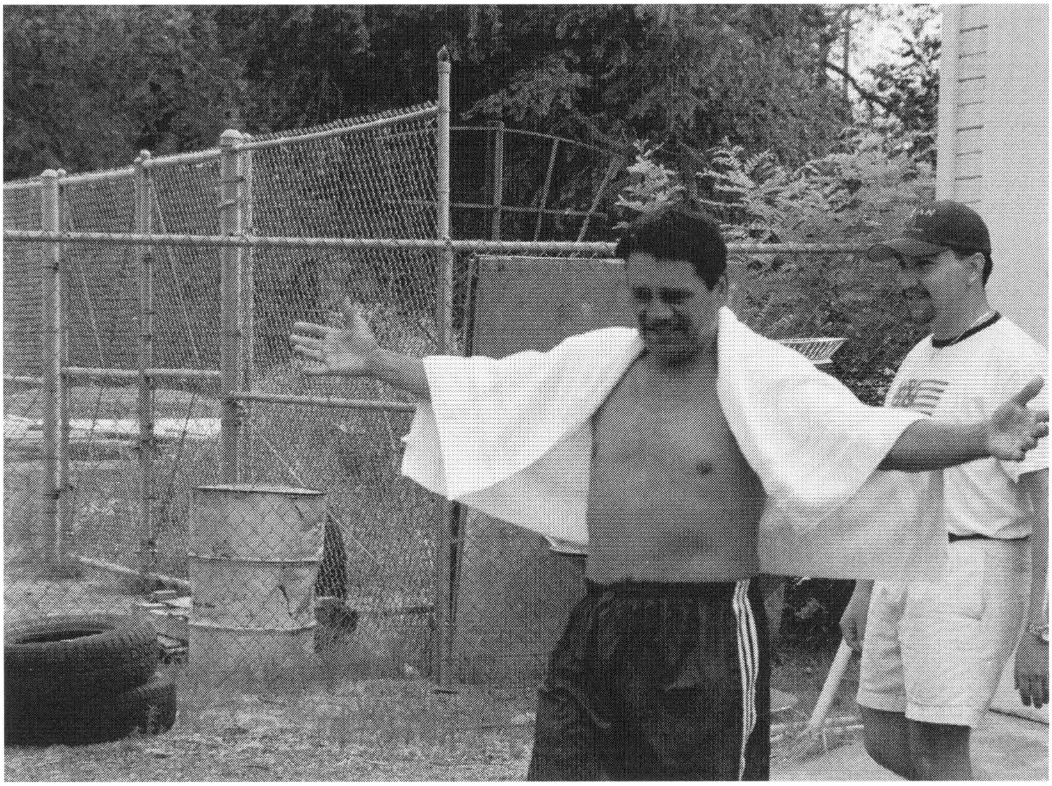

Again he must sign posters and boxing equipment for the Casino.

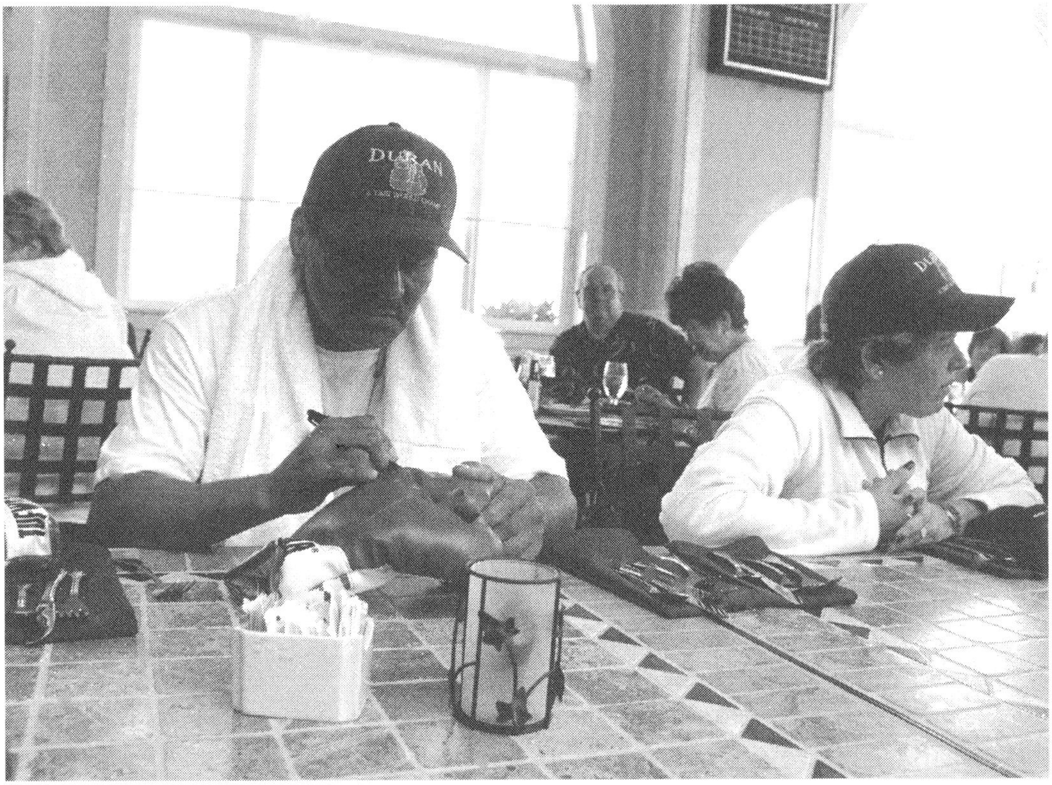

While Duran has been in training, so has Goossen. He is in excellent shape and anxious for the fight. Duran is one of his heros but he has no problem fighting him.

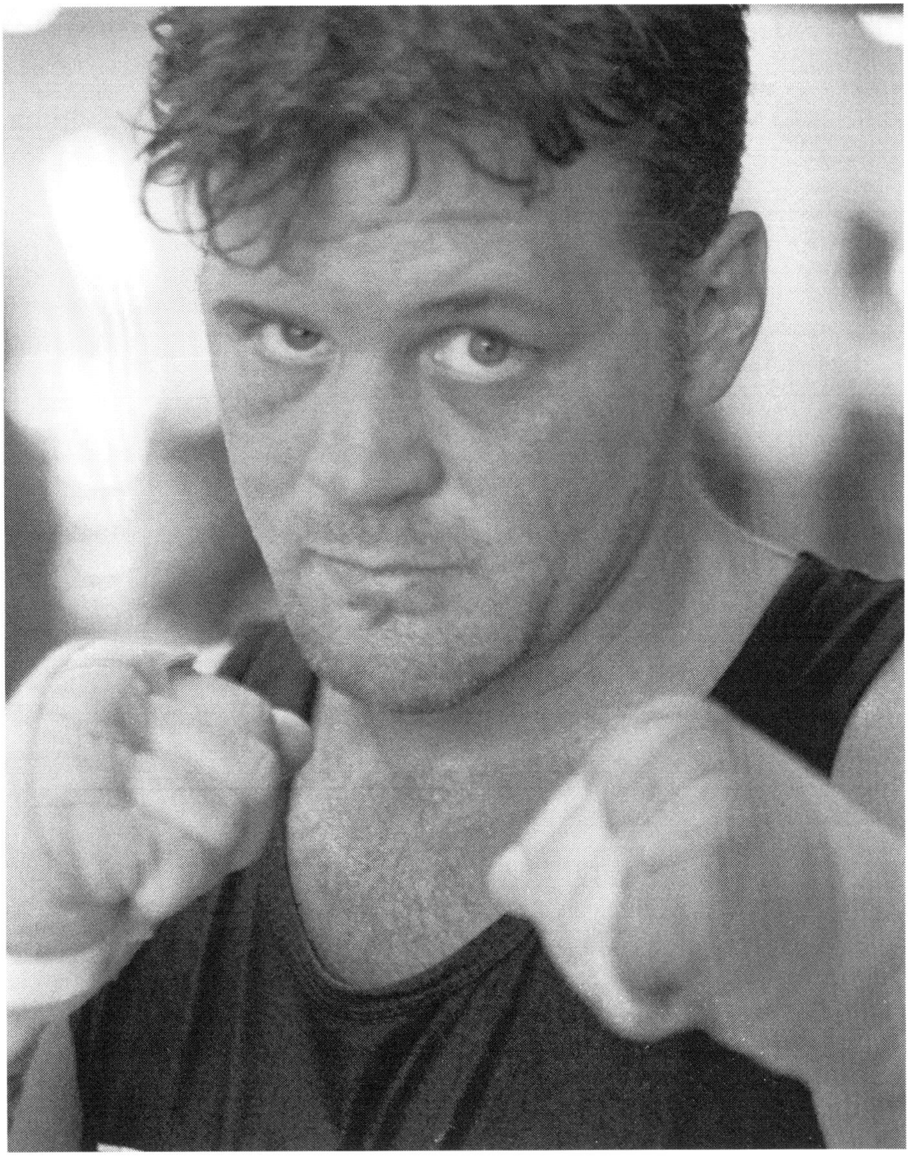

There are many details that must be arranged before a fight. The local taylor puts together Duran's trunk and robe.

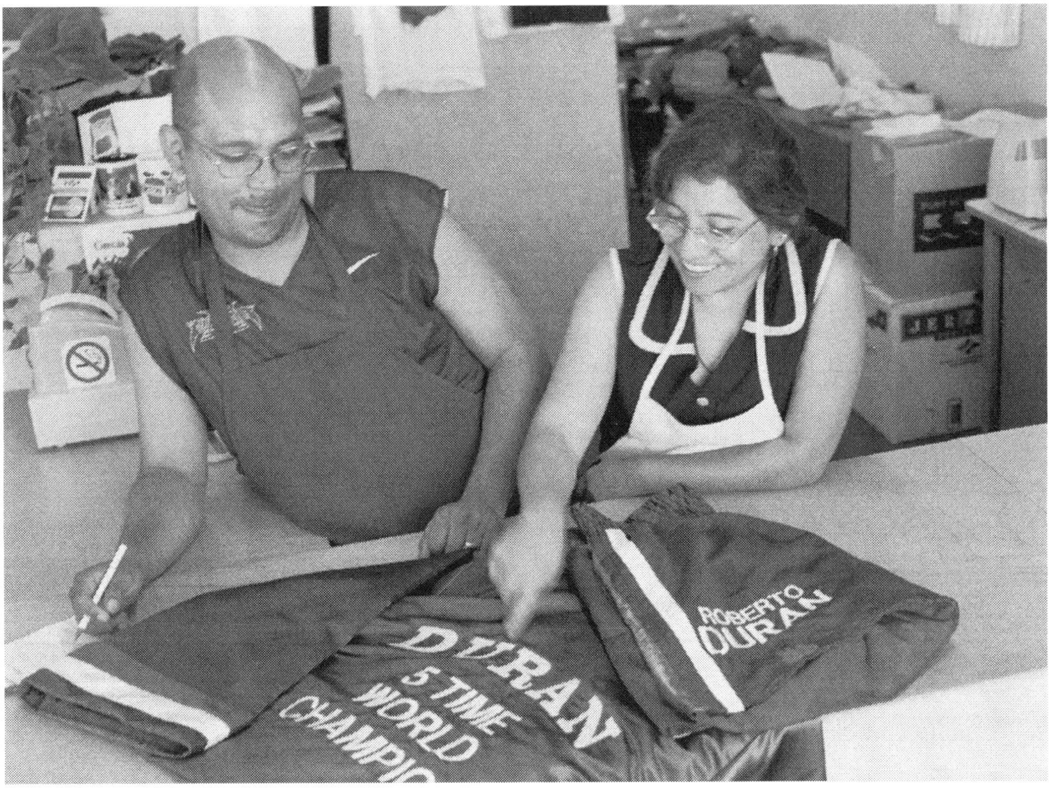
DURAN
5 TIME
WORLD
ROBERTO
DURAN

Duran has great legs and keeps his feet hard on the canvass when throwing punches.

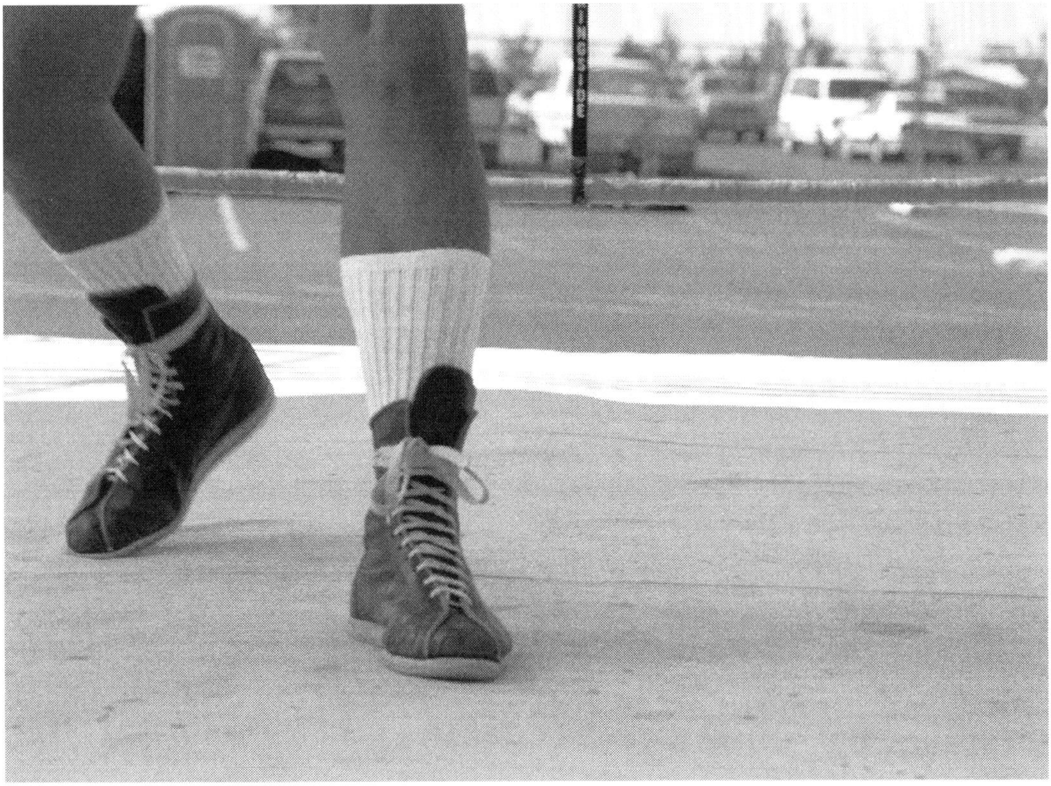

P.J. Goossen arrives with his dad, Pat, several days before the fight.

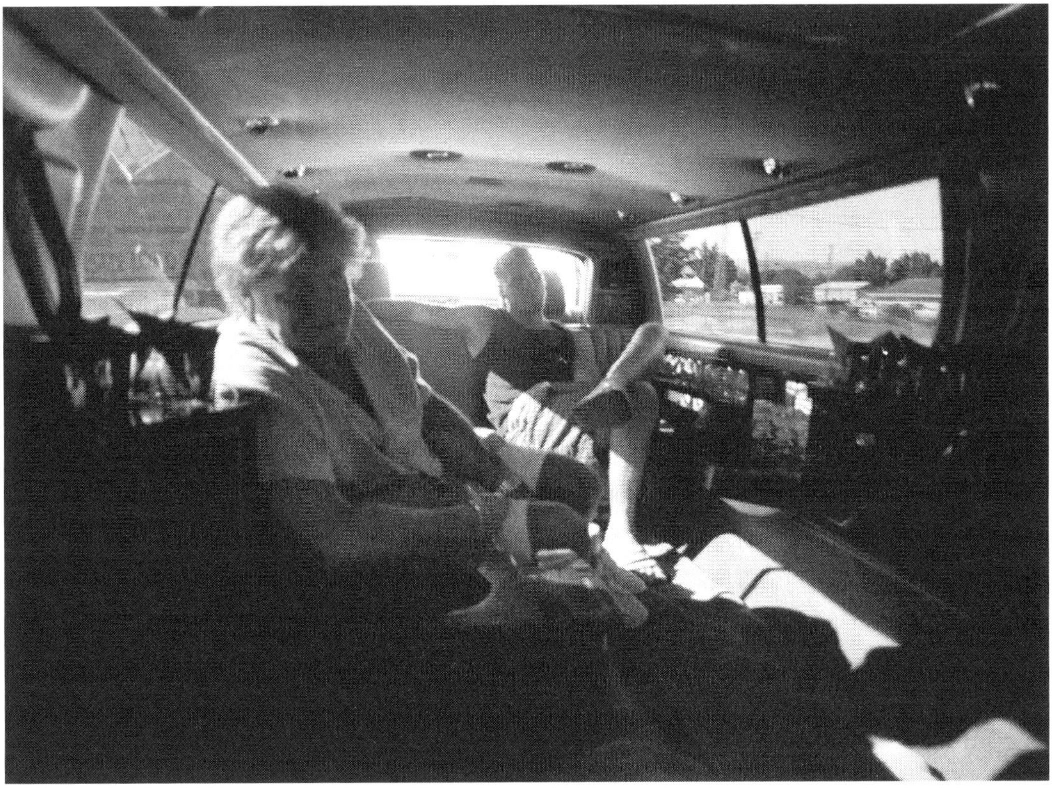

He starts to settle in with his entourage.

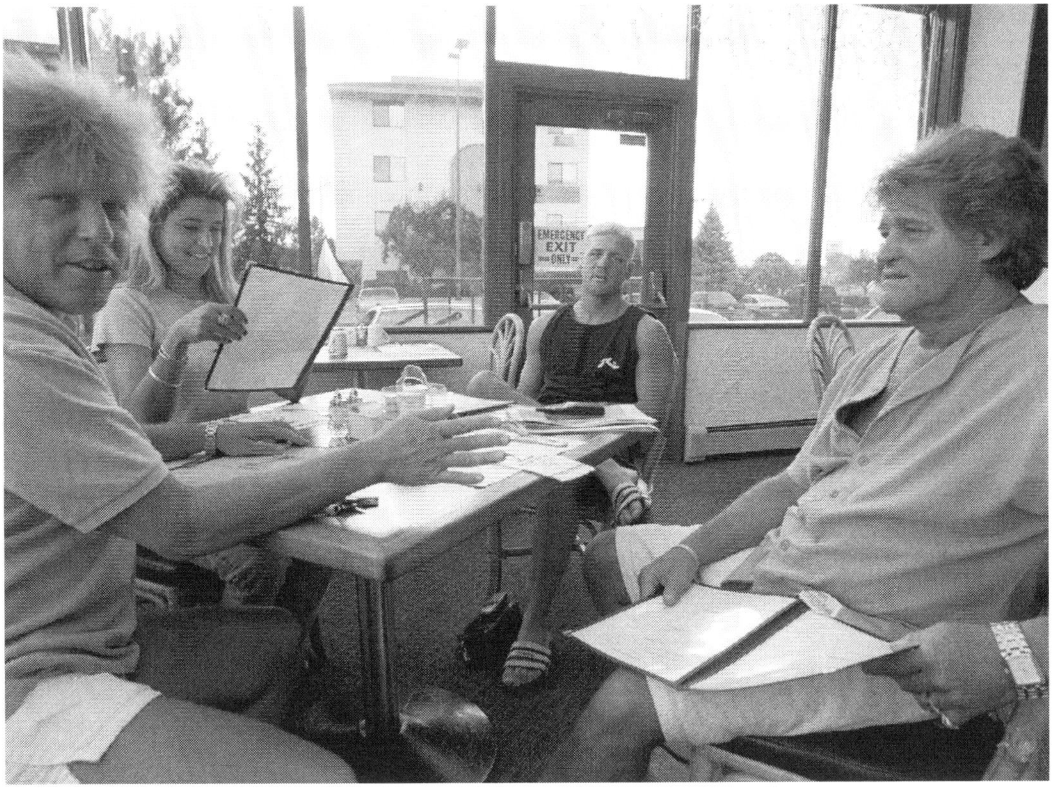
EMERGENCY
EXIT
ONLY

The reporters show up in force. They talk to anyone they can. Nestor gives his take on the fight.

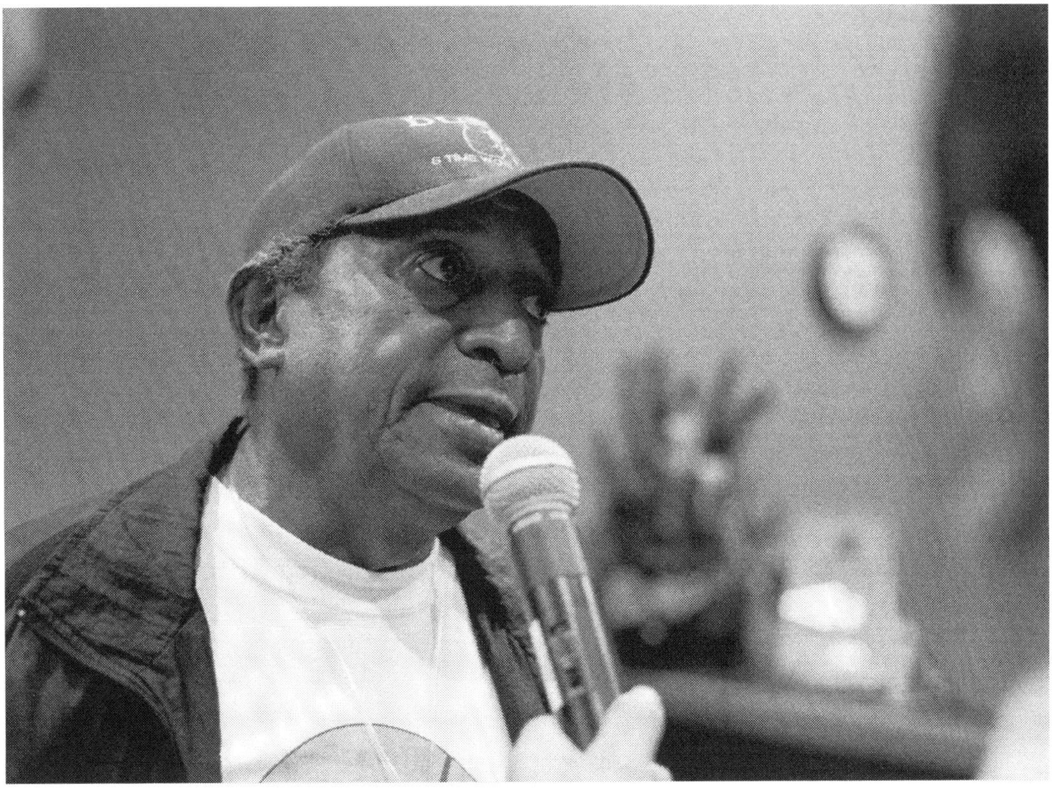

Anthony gets cornered at the hotel.

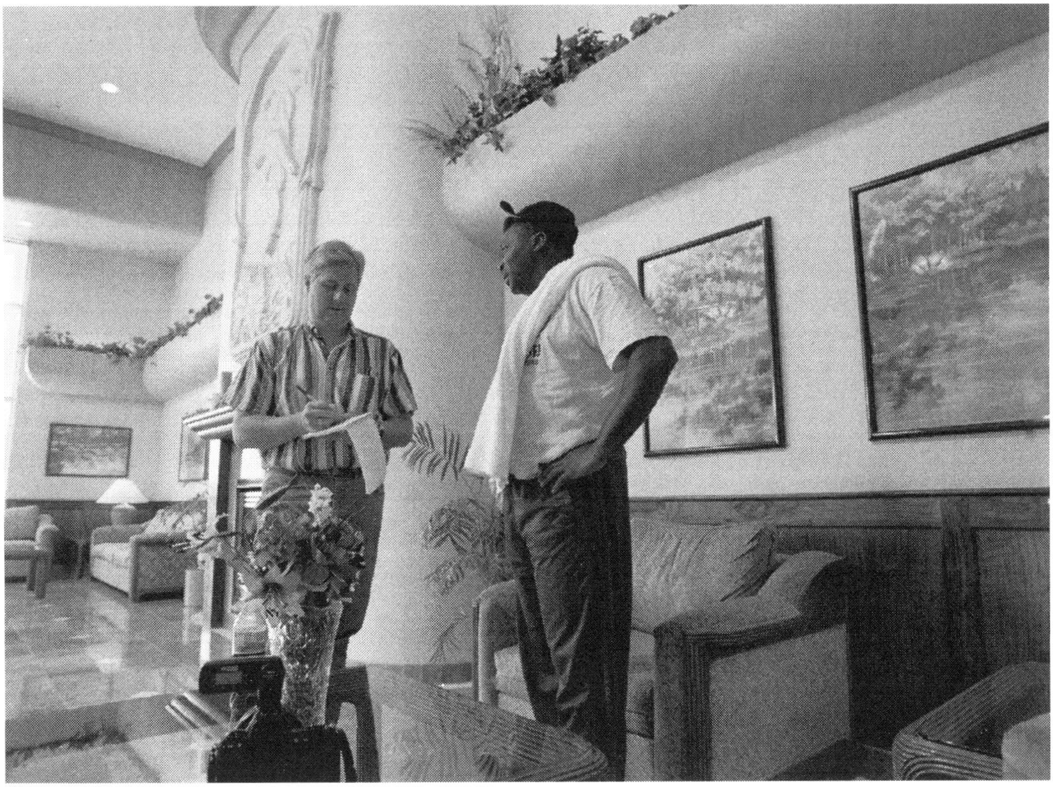

Duran checks out the ring. He likes fighting outside.

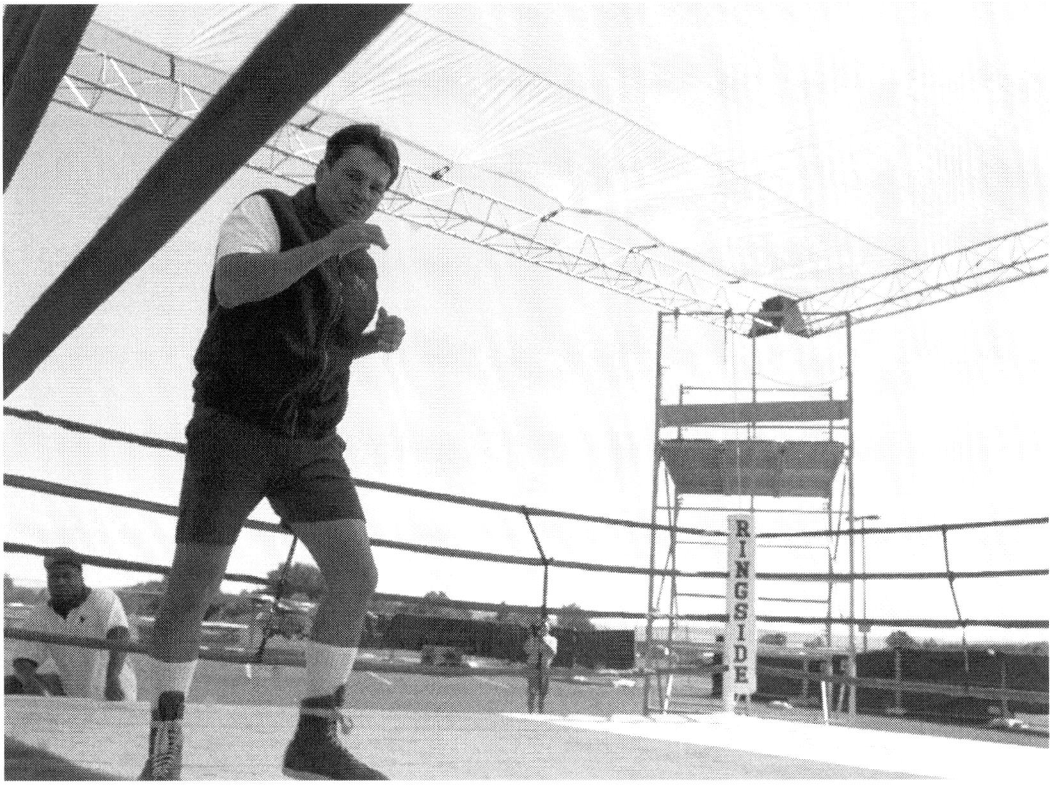
RINGSIDE

The last press conference is given.

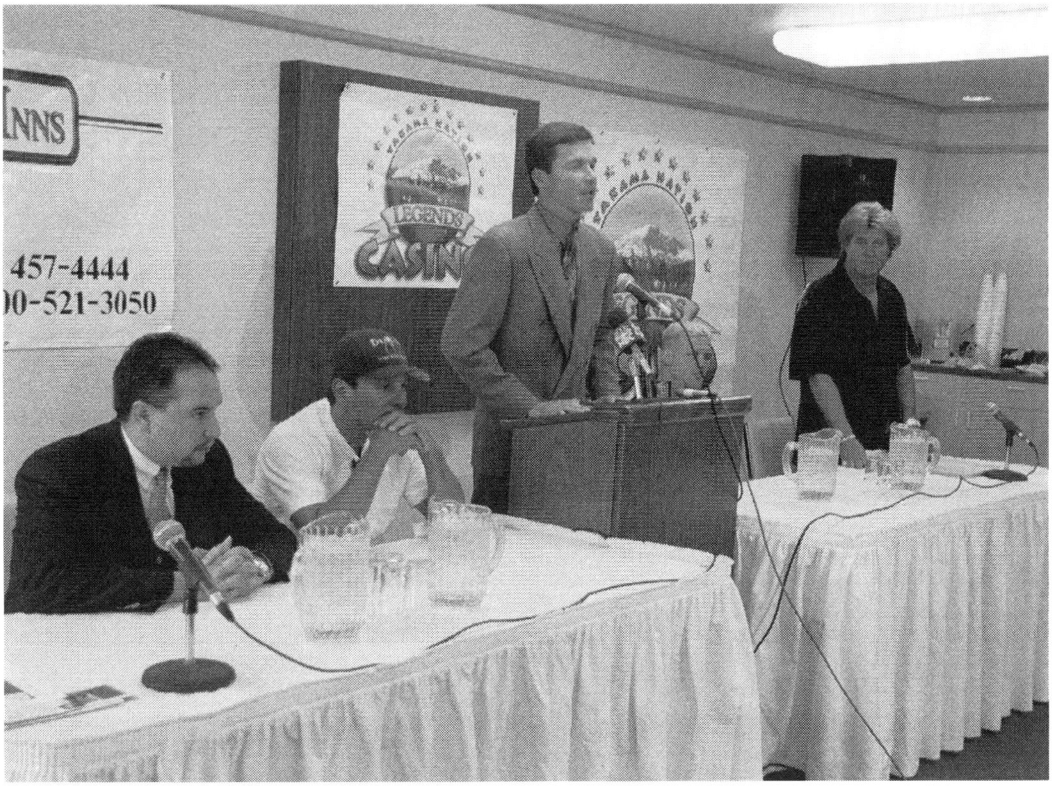

INNS
457-4444
00-521-3050
LEGENDS

Weighins are always fun. It's chance for all fighters to size up each other and for various people in the fight game to get together. P.J. notices that something is wrong with Duran's finger.

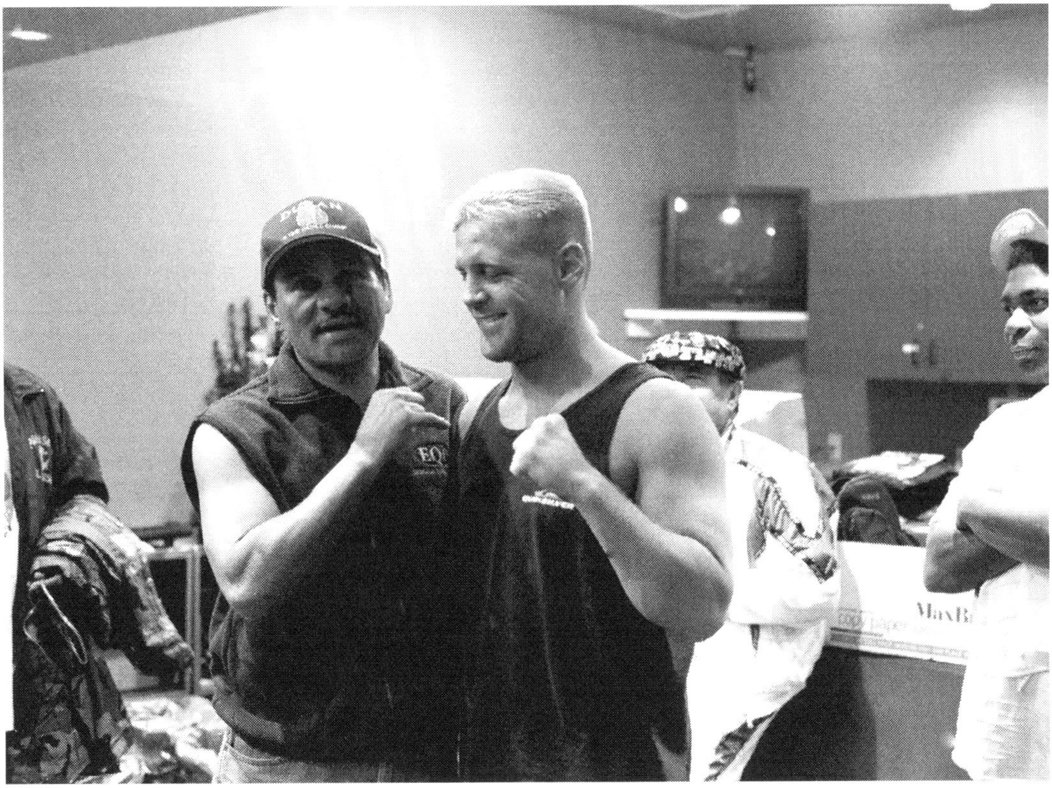

Goossen is in great shape.

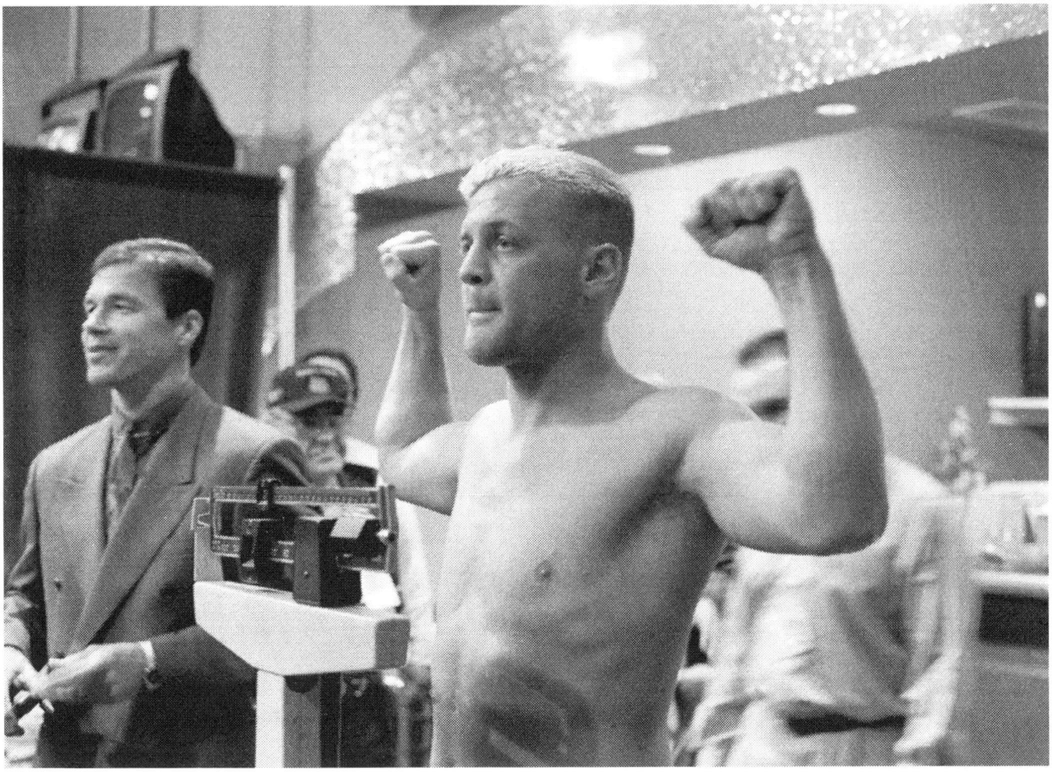

One final picture and the fight is on.

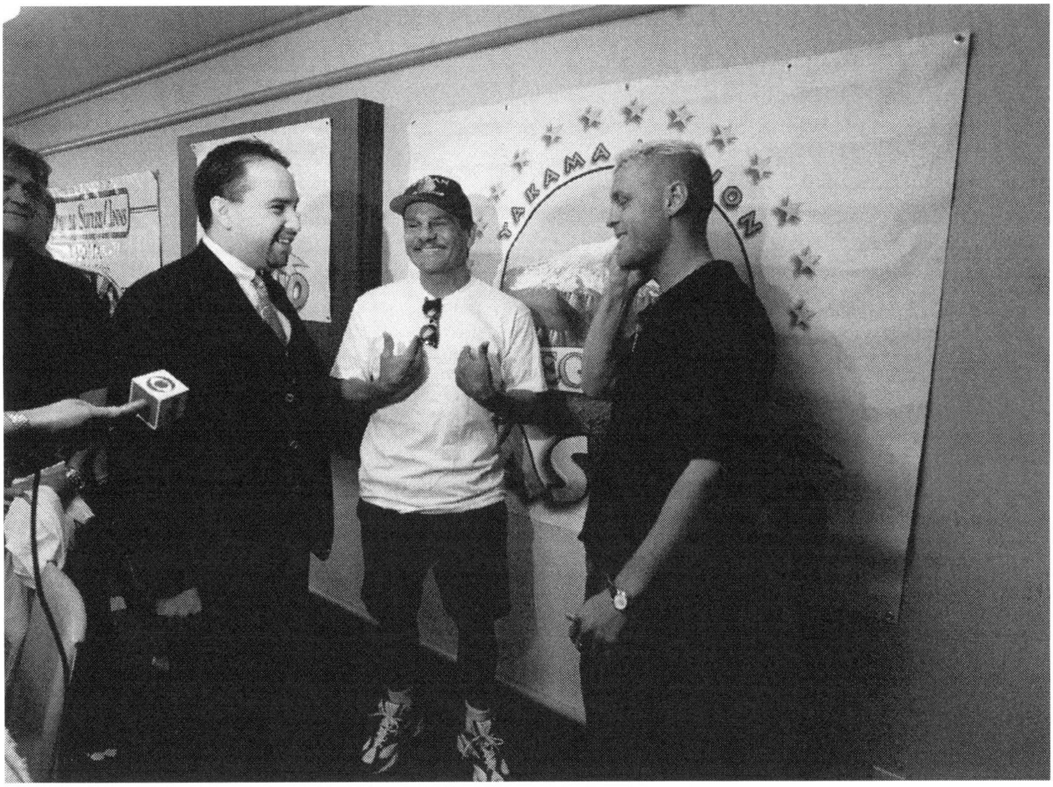

Duran warms up. He has spent the entire night eating and he looks slow and sluggish. He had only to eat moderately one last night, but he could not resist the food.

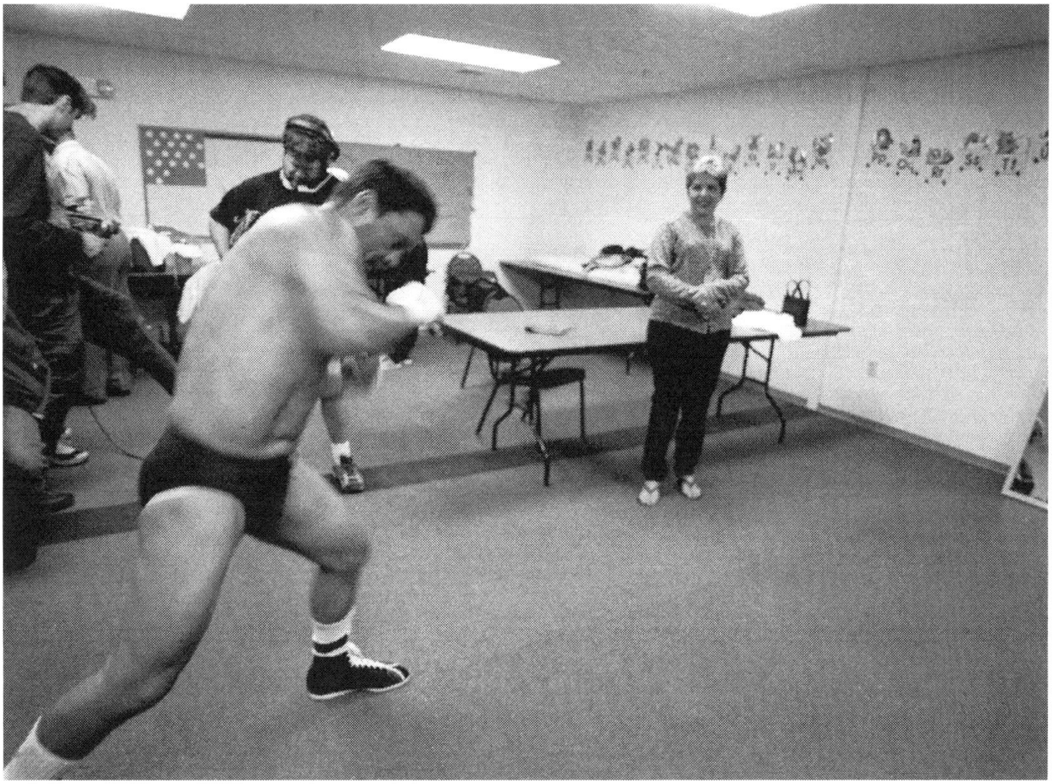

Nestor is very careful lacing up Duran's glove.

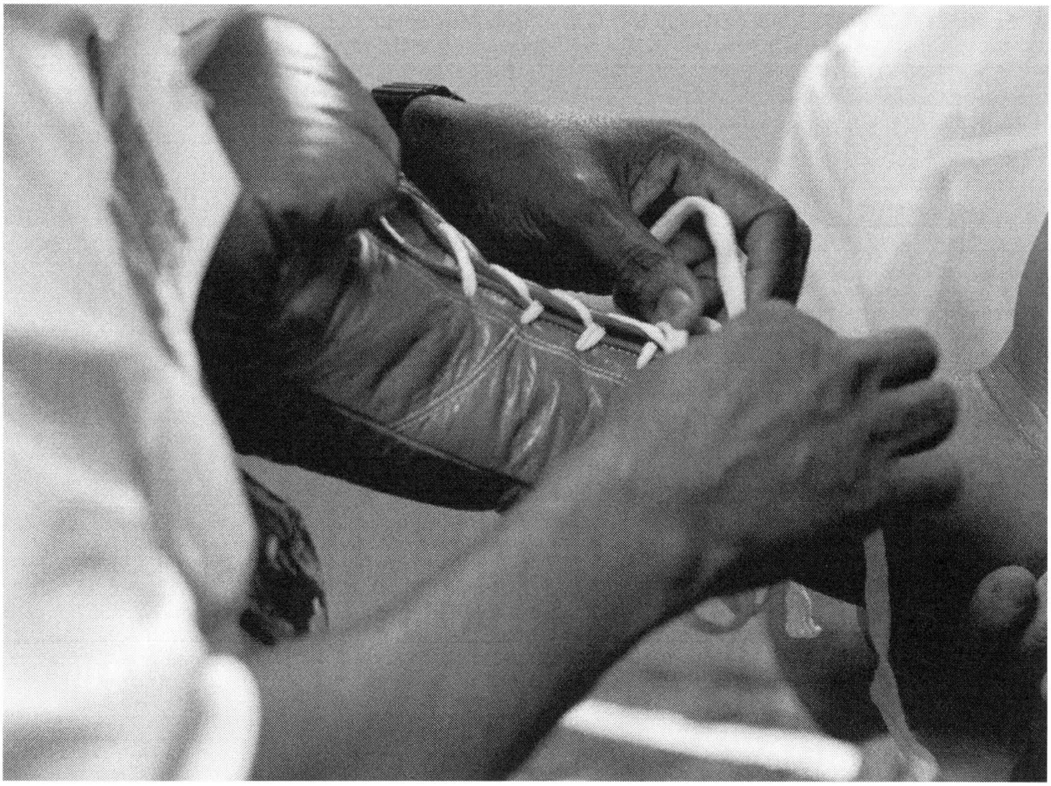

Duran throws a few rights to make sure his finger is comfortable.

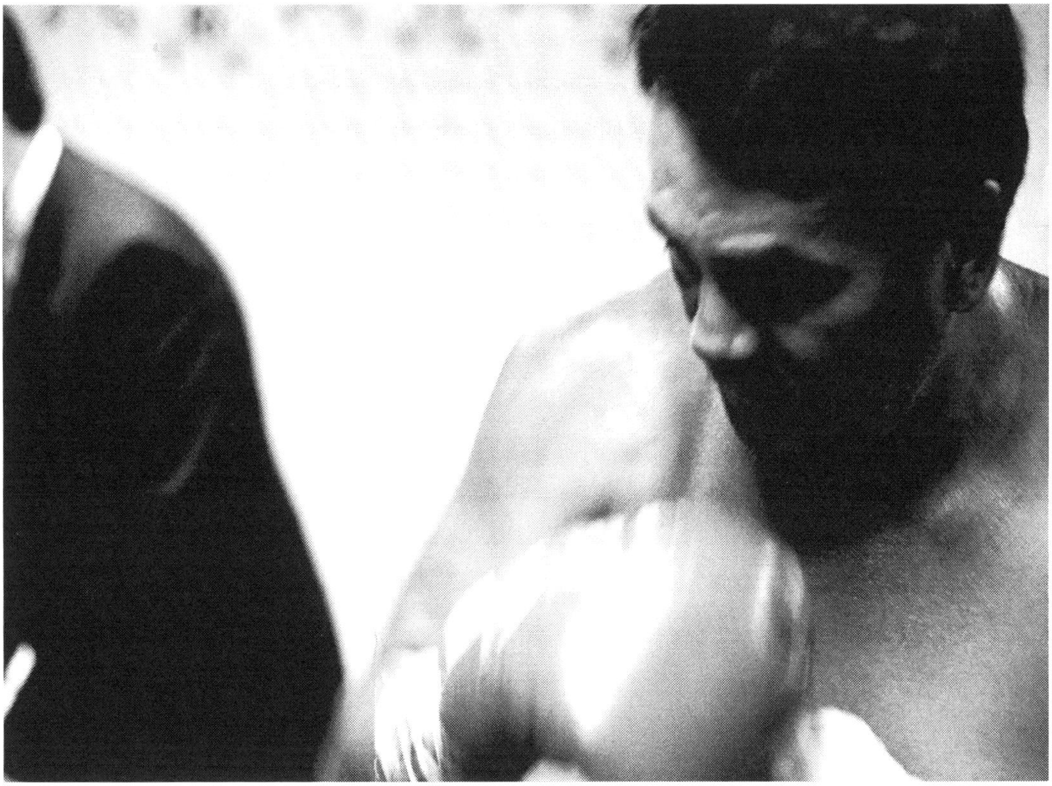

Duran has worked up a sweat and is ready.

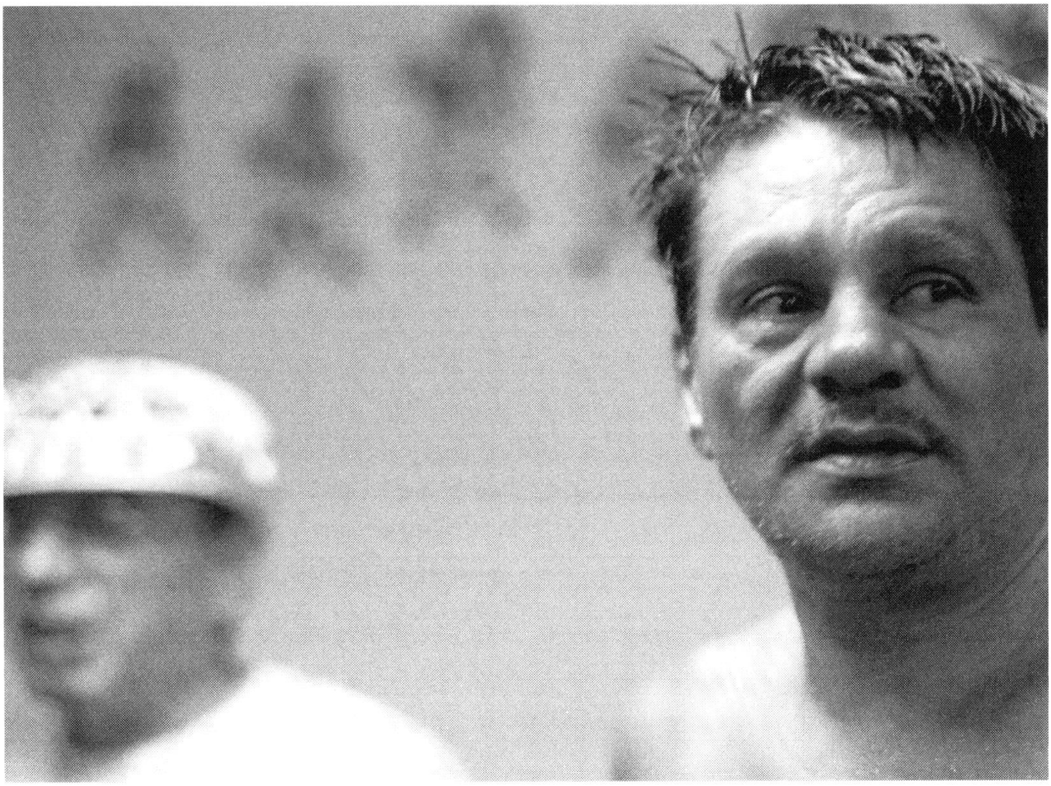

Admirers mob Duran on the way to the ring.

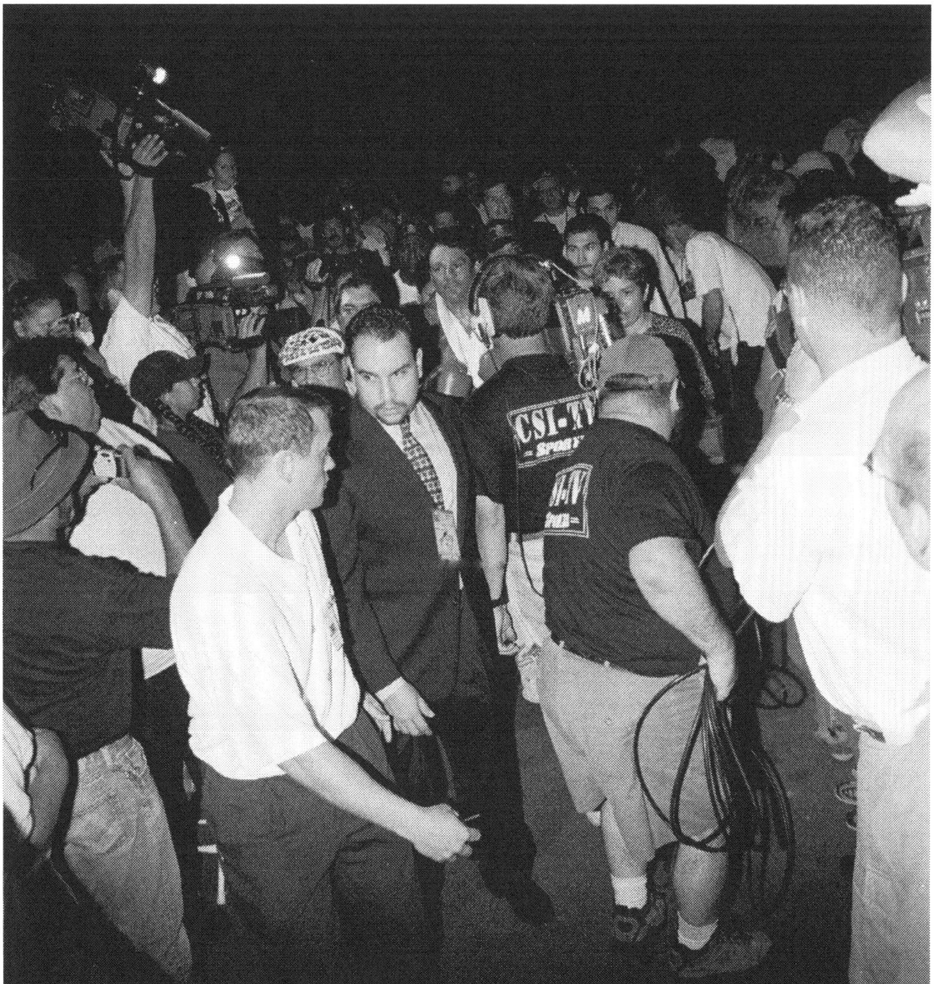
CSI-TV

The champion is announced.

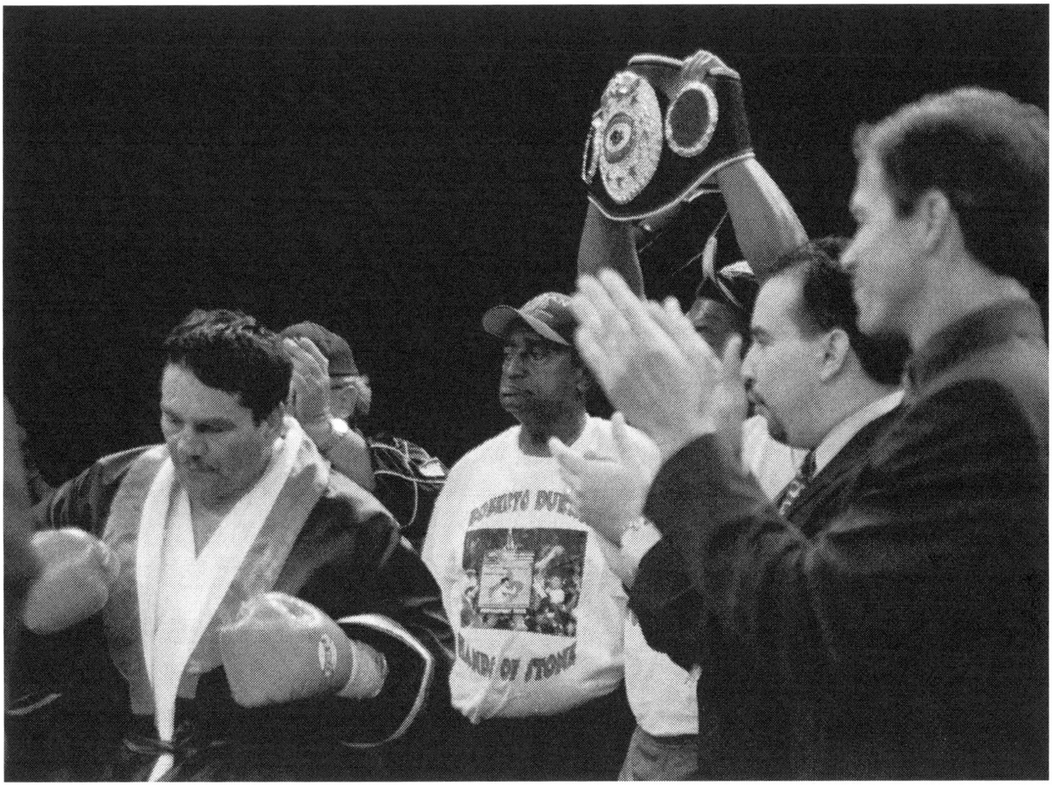

Goossen looks good.

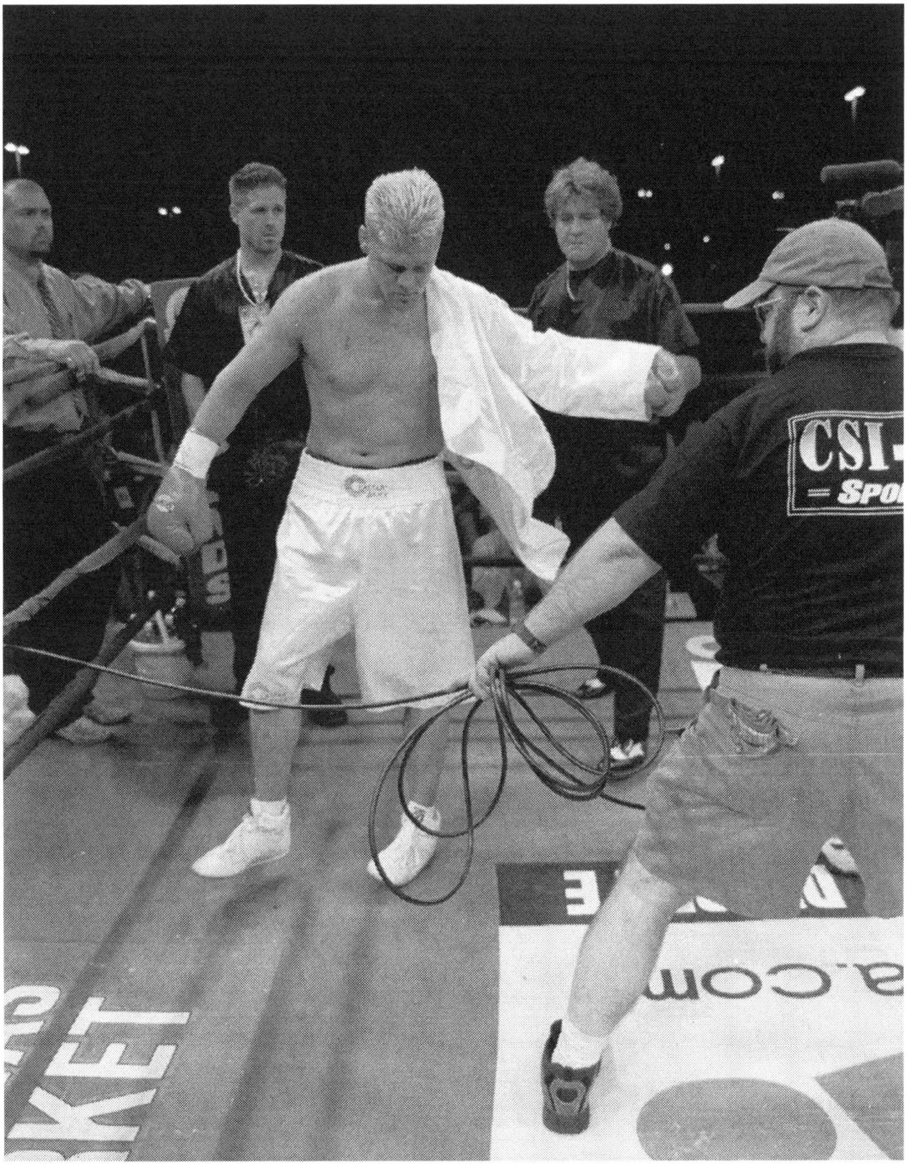
CSI-

Jeff Conors does the announcing.

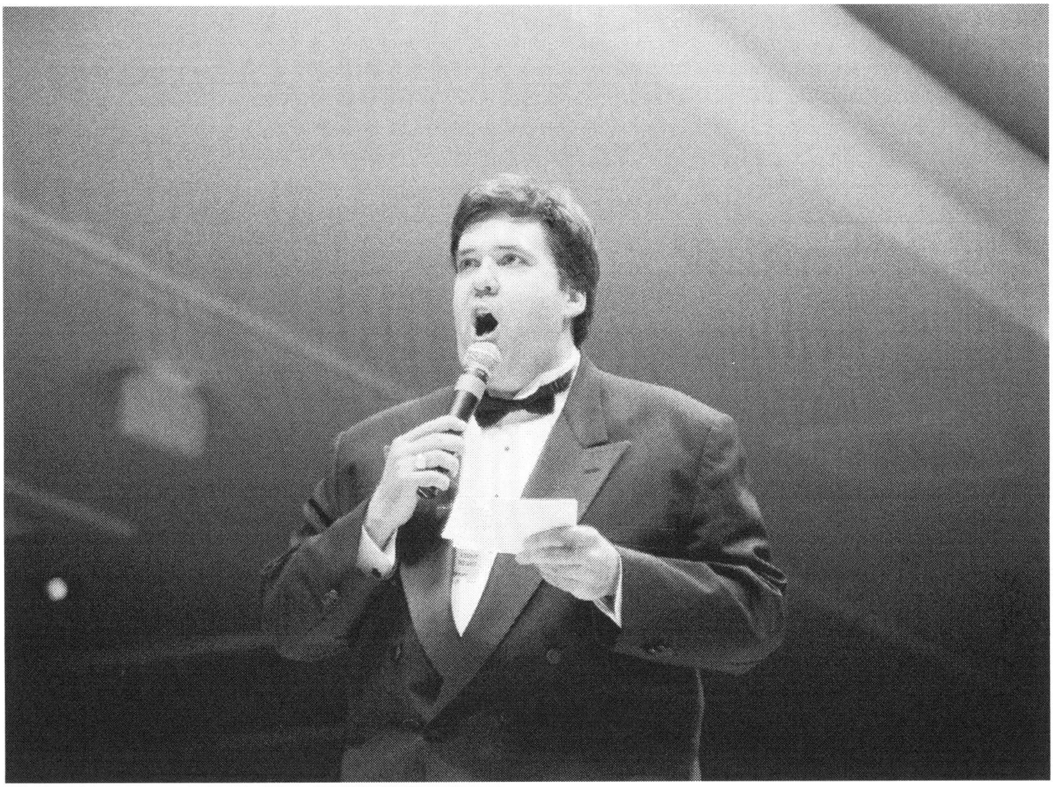

Both fighters come out swinging trying to dominate the other.

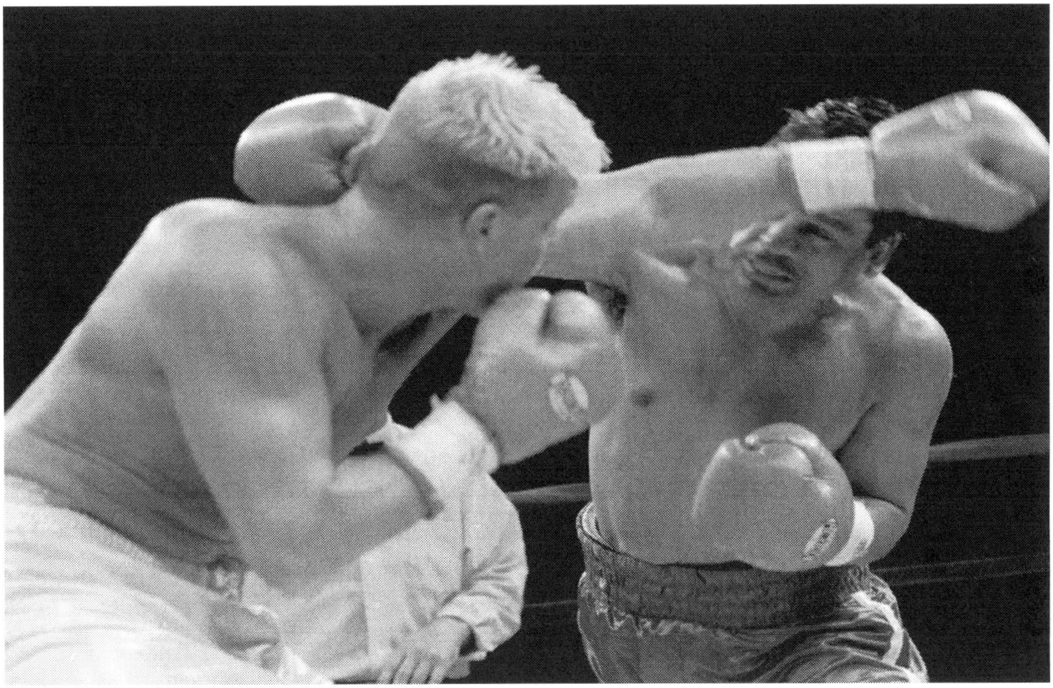

The extra skin from his weight loss is evident on Durn.

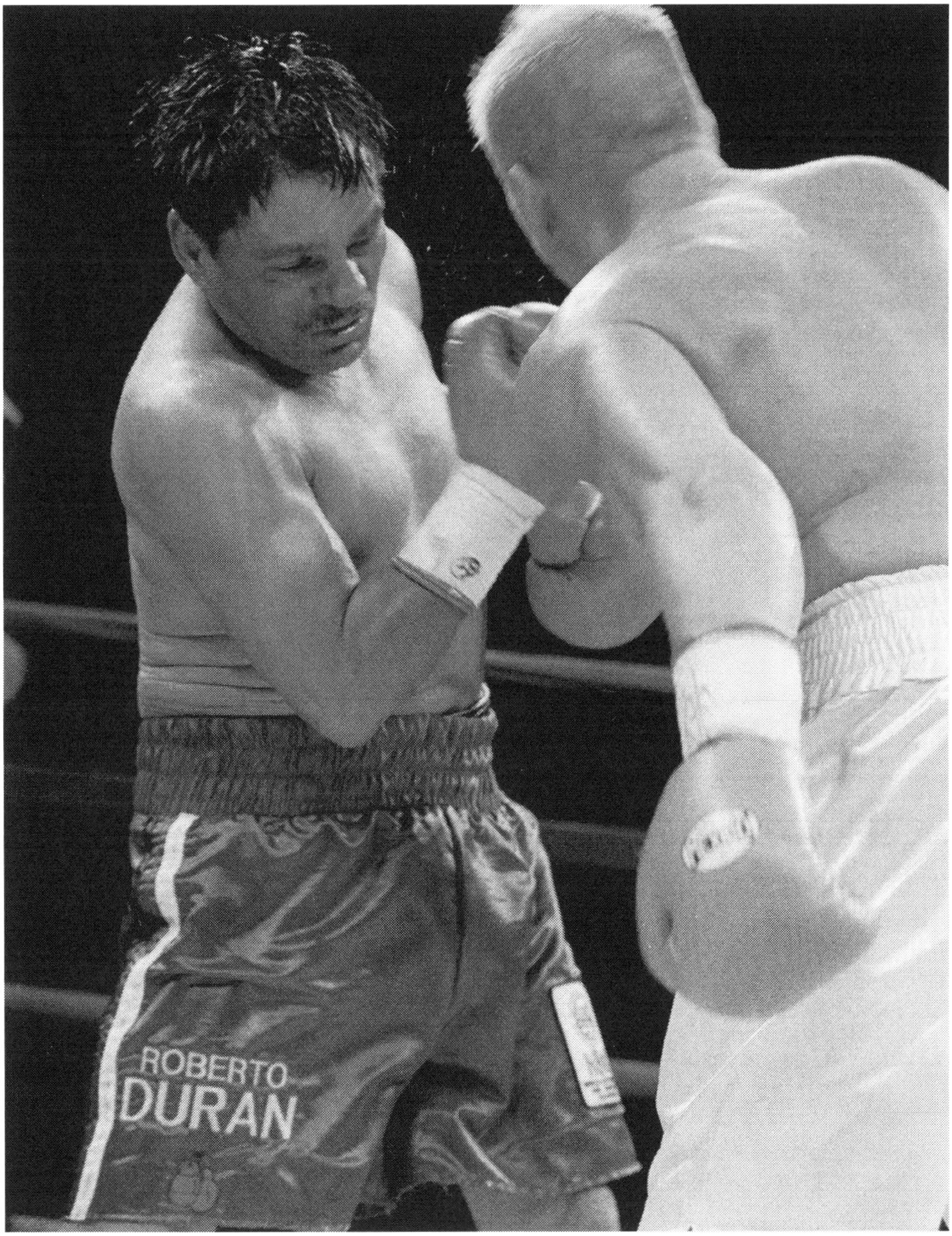
ROBERTO
DURAN

In the opening rounds, Duran remains slow. He looked like the old Duran during the last weeks of training, but the food is bogging him down.

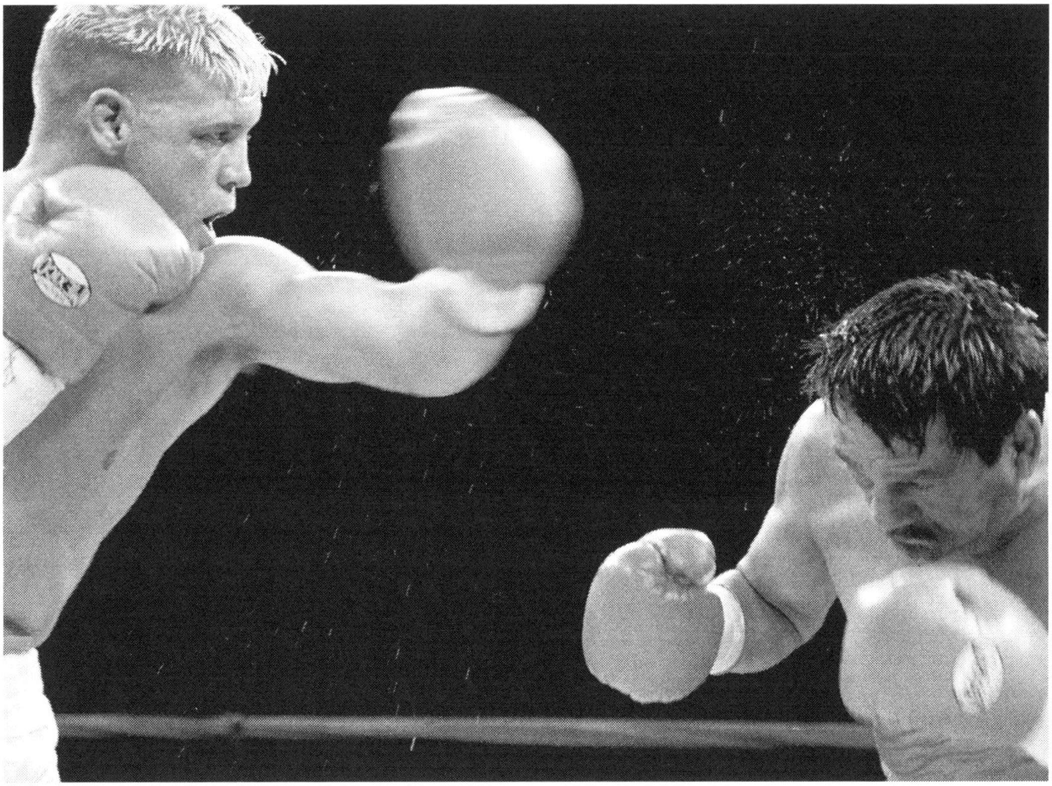

As the fight continues, Duran fights his way back into shape. He looks better and faster each round while Goossen starts to tire.

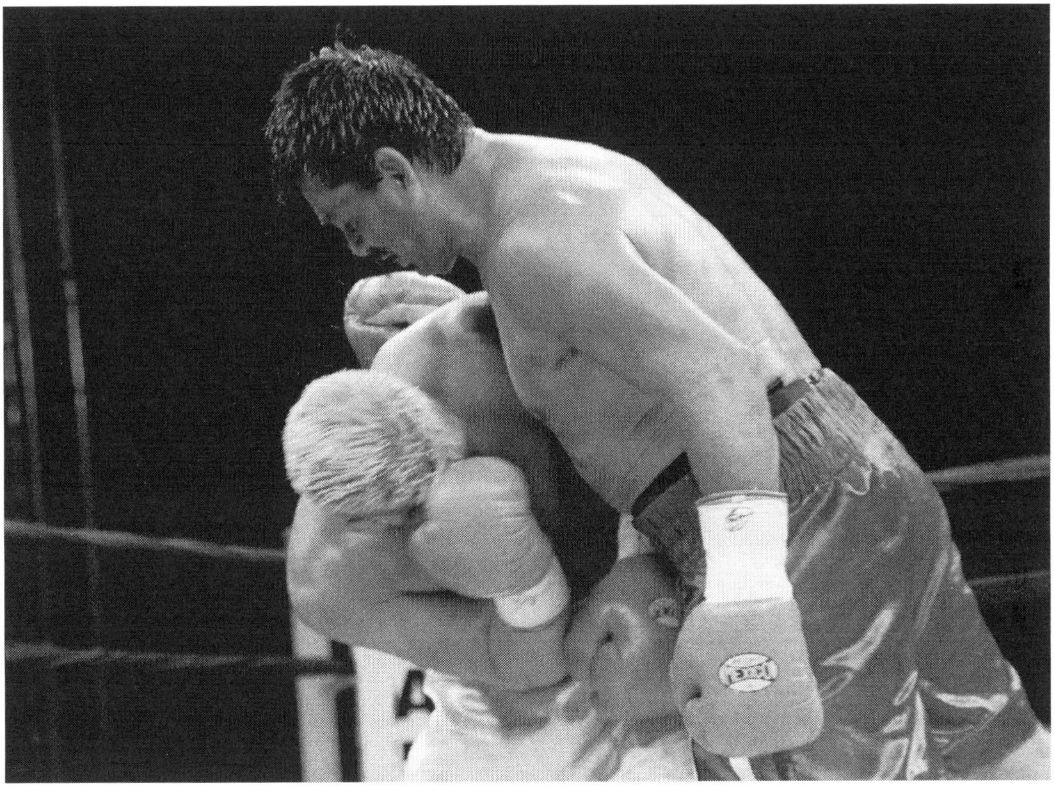

Duran looks like his old self - a much older version of his old self.

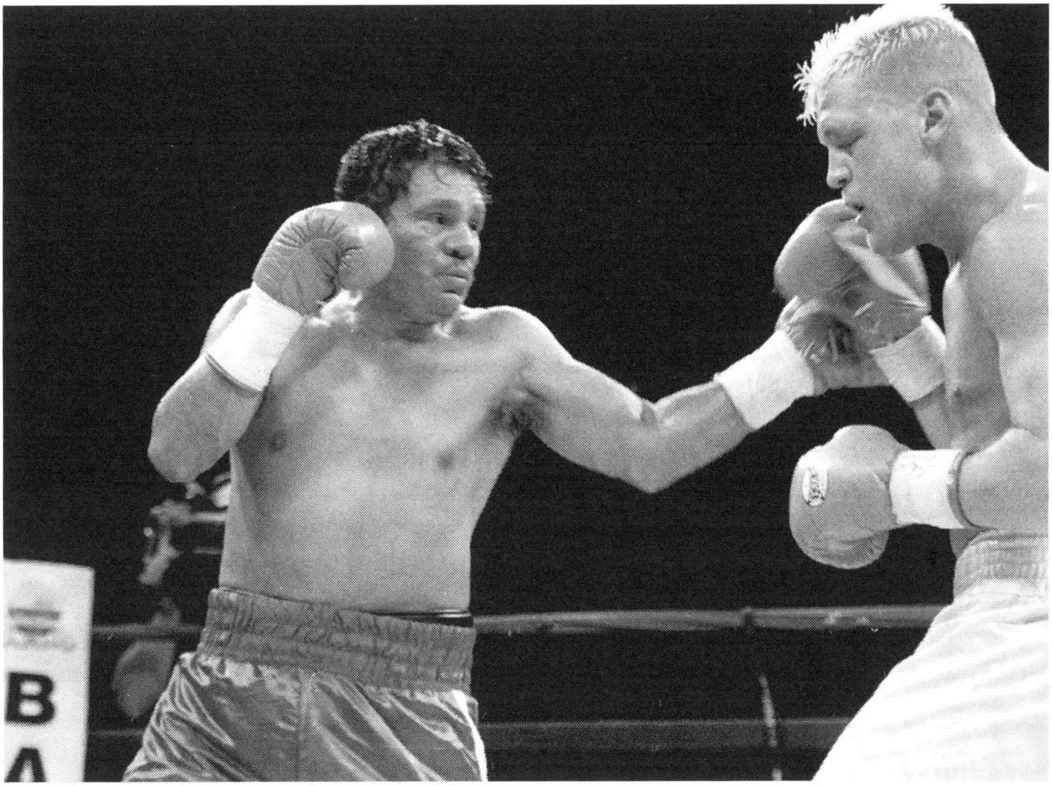

Duran knows the fight will be a long one. Goossen refuses to quit.

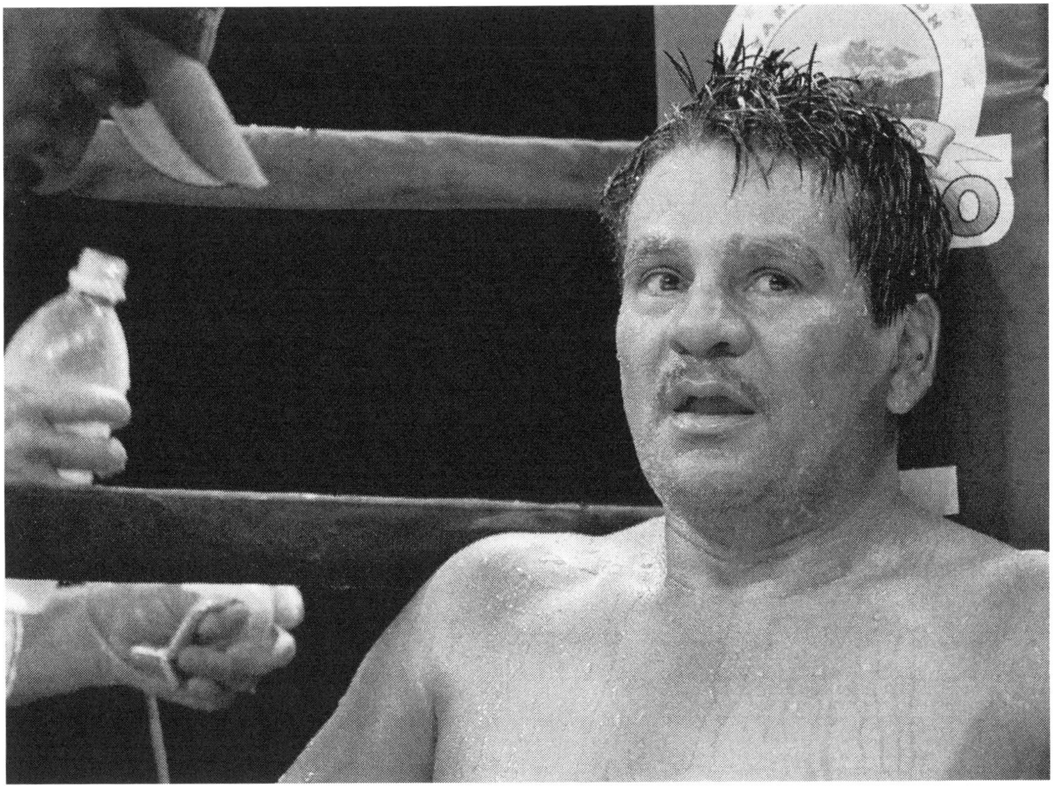

e

Goossen wants to knock Duran out, to make a statement, show that he is more than a club fighter.

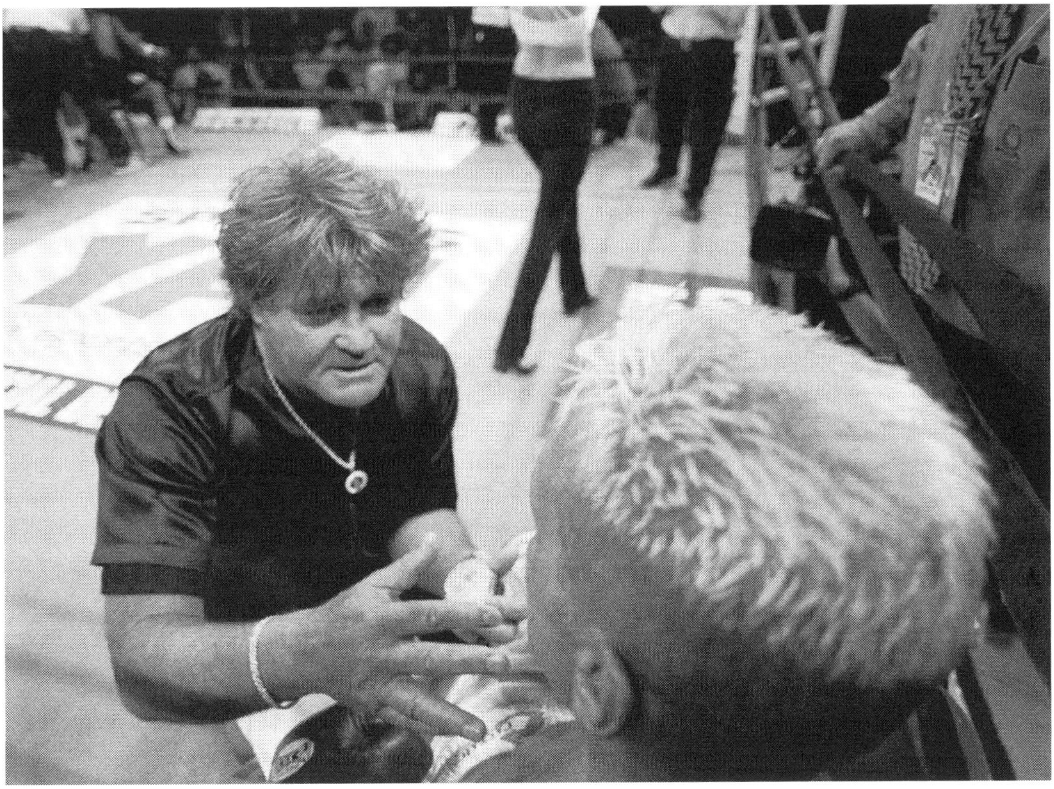

Duran knows he has taken charge. The grimace returns and he goes for the knockout, but Goossen will not go down.

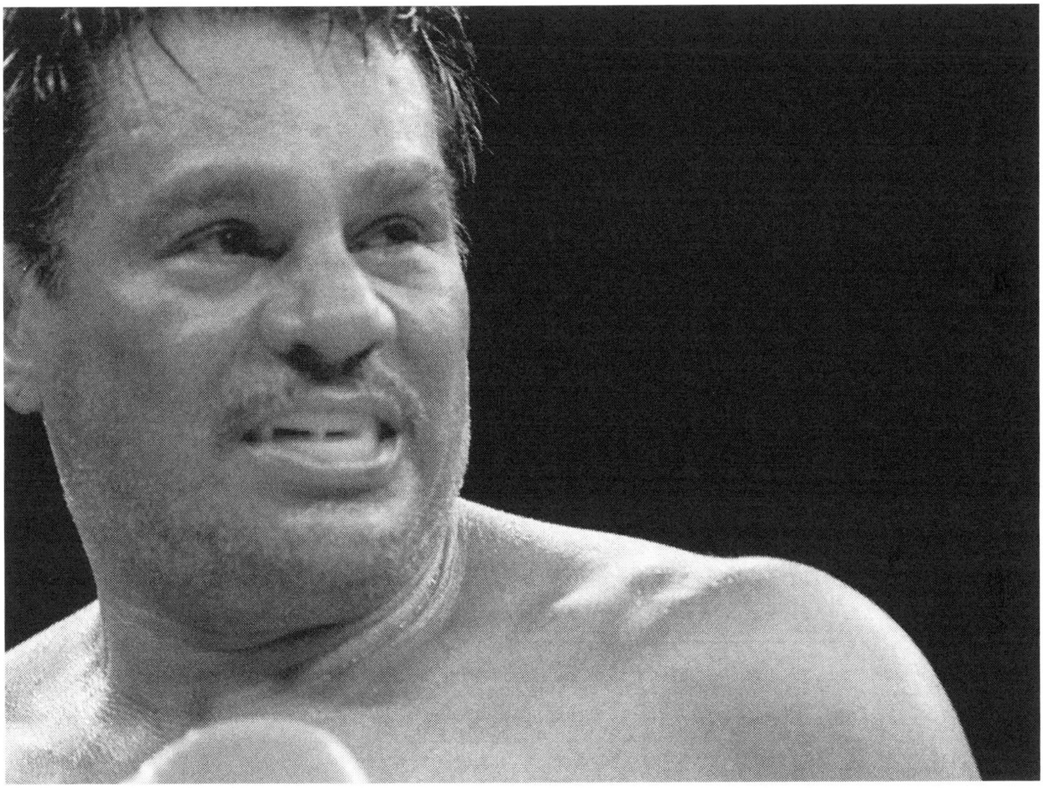

Duran feels good and congratulates Goossen.

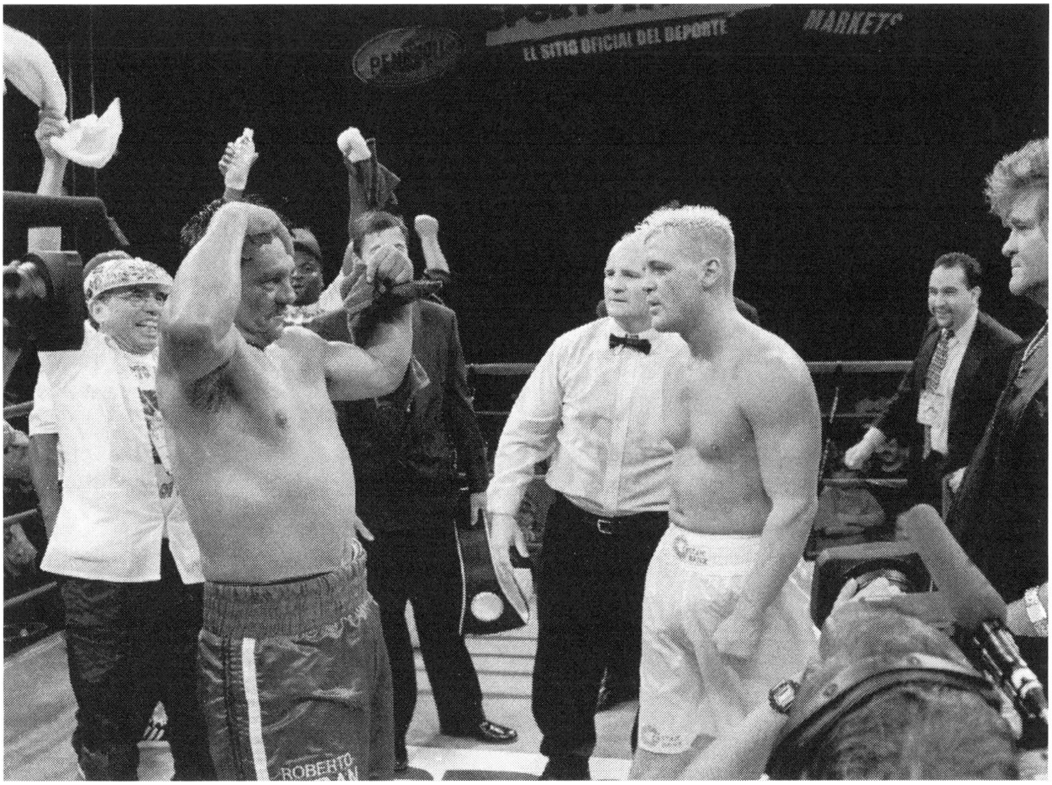
EL SITIO OFICIAL DEL DEPORTE
MARKETS
ROBERTO

Goossen also feels good and confident. Getting a decision against a champion is always difficult.

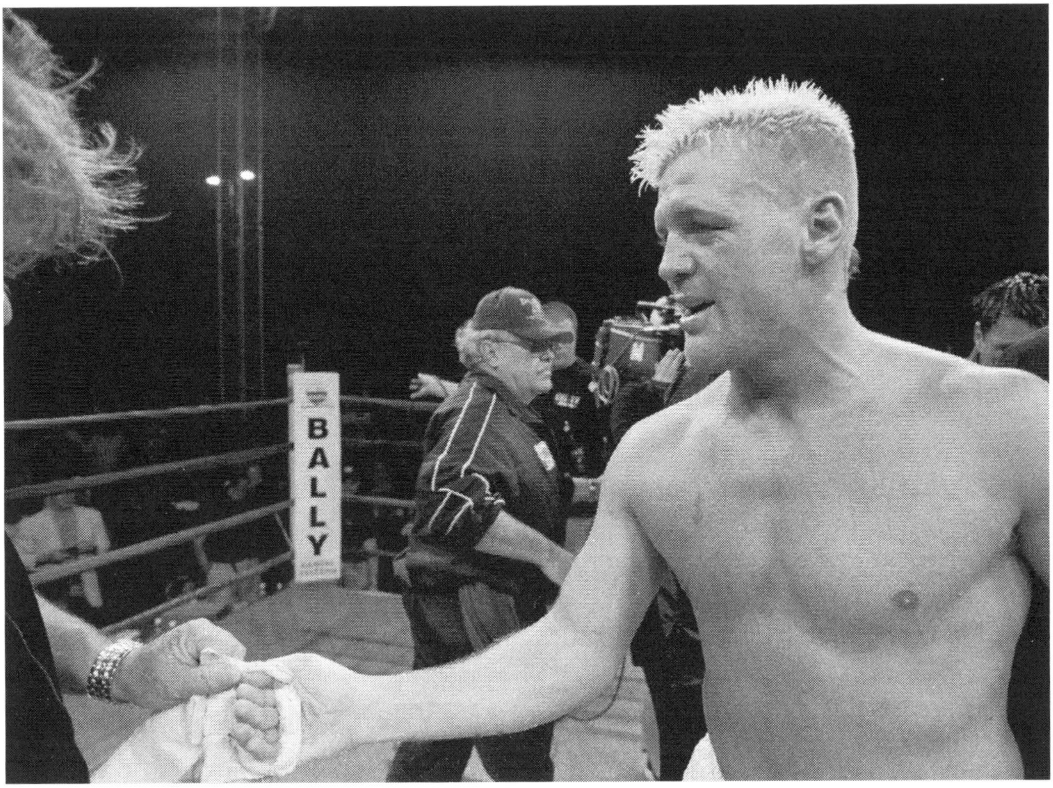
BALLY

Duran wins his last title fight by unanimous decision

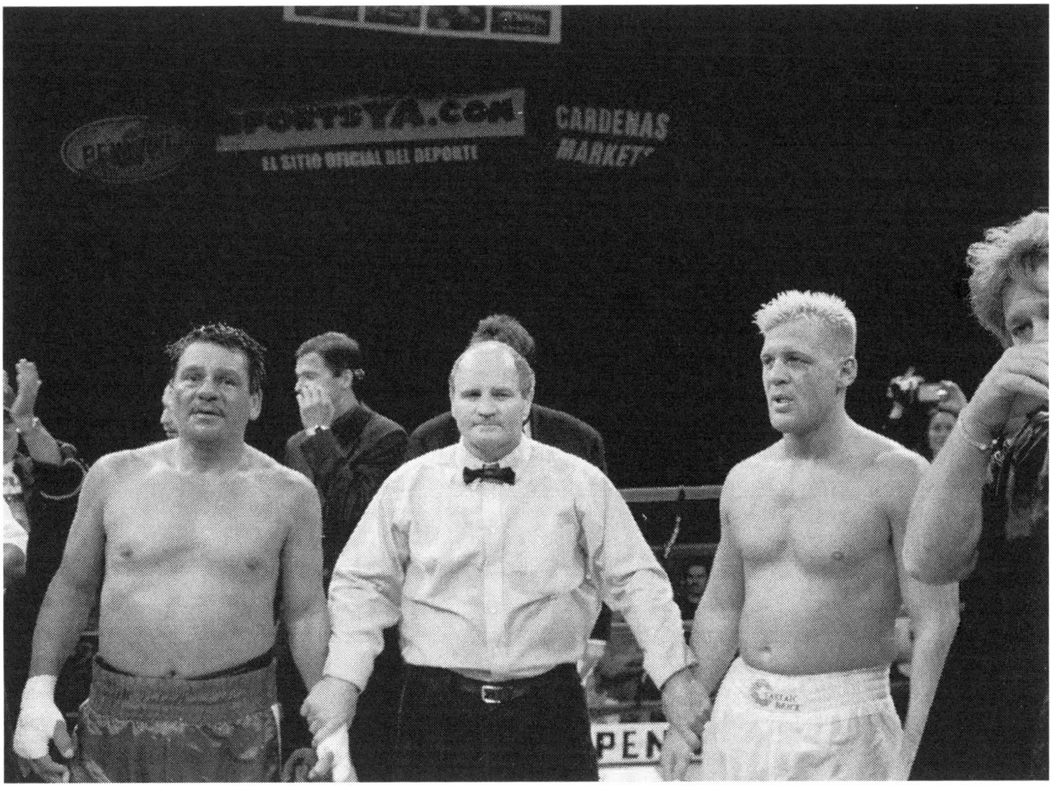

CARDENAS
EL SITIO OFICIAL DEL DEPORTE

Goossen is not happy with the decision.

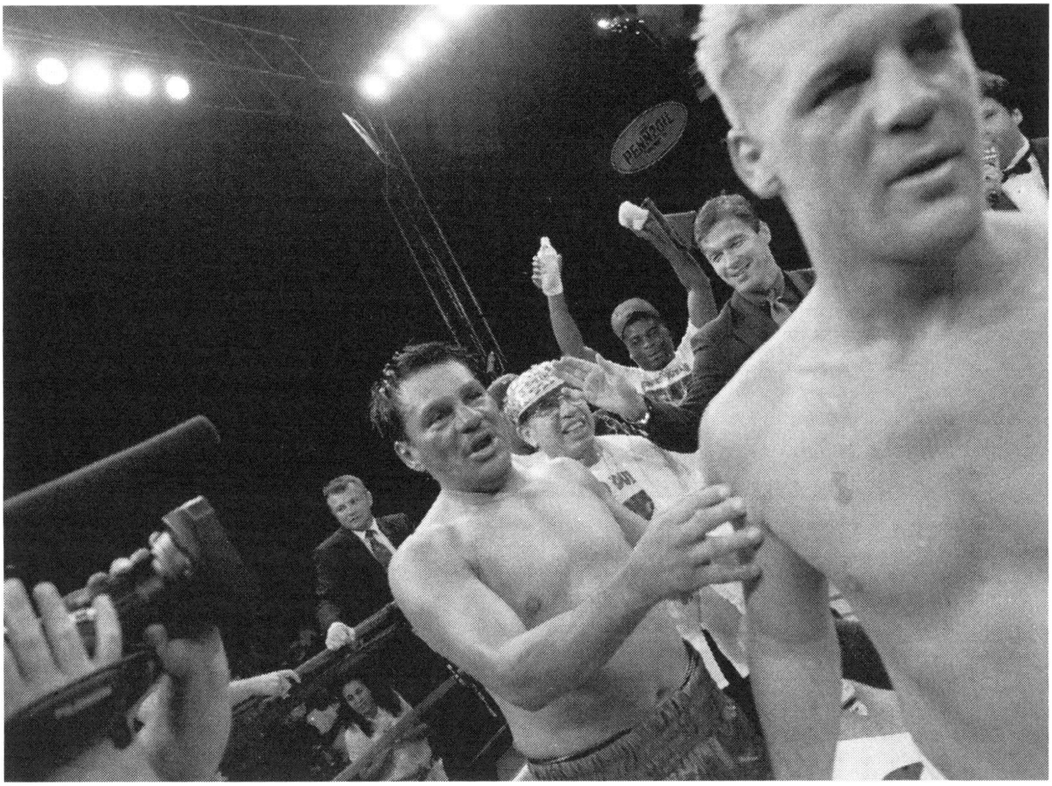

Duran, back to the lovable teddy bear he becomes between fights, again thanks him for a great fight. Goossen is drawn in by is charm.

PENNZOIL
SPORTSYA.COM
EL SITIO OFICIAL DEL DEPORTE
CARDENAS
MARKE
NZOIL
DURAN

Duran struts around the ring and enjoys the crowd.

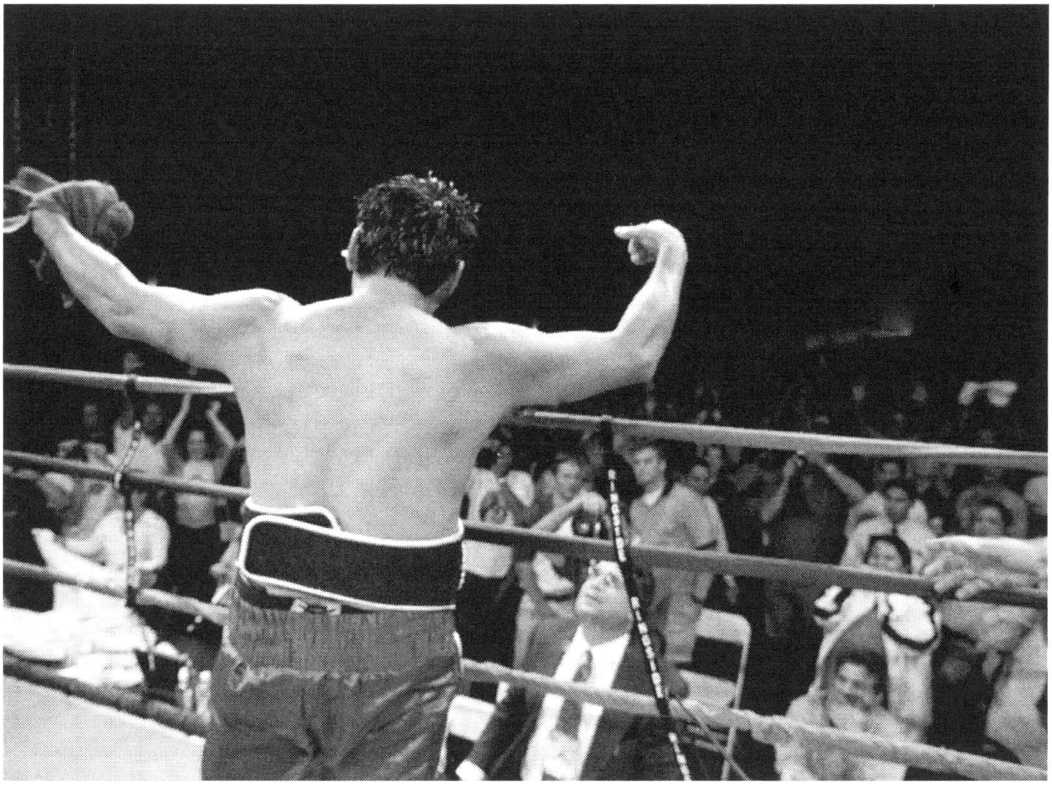

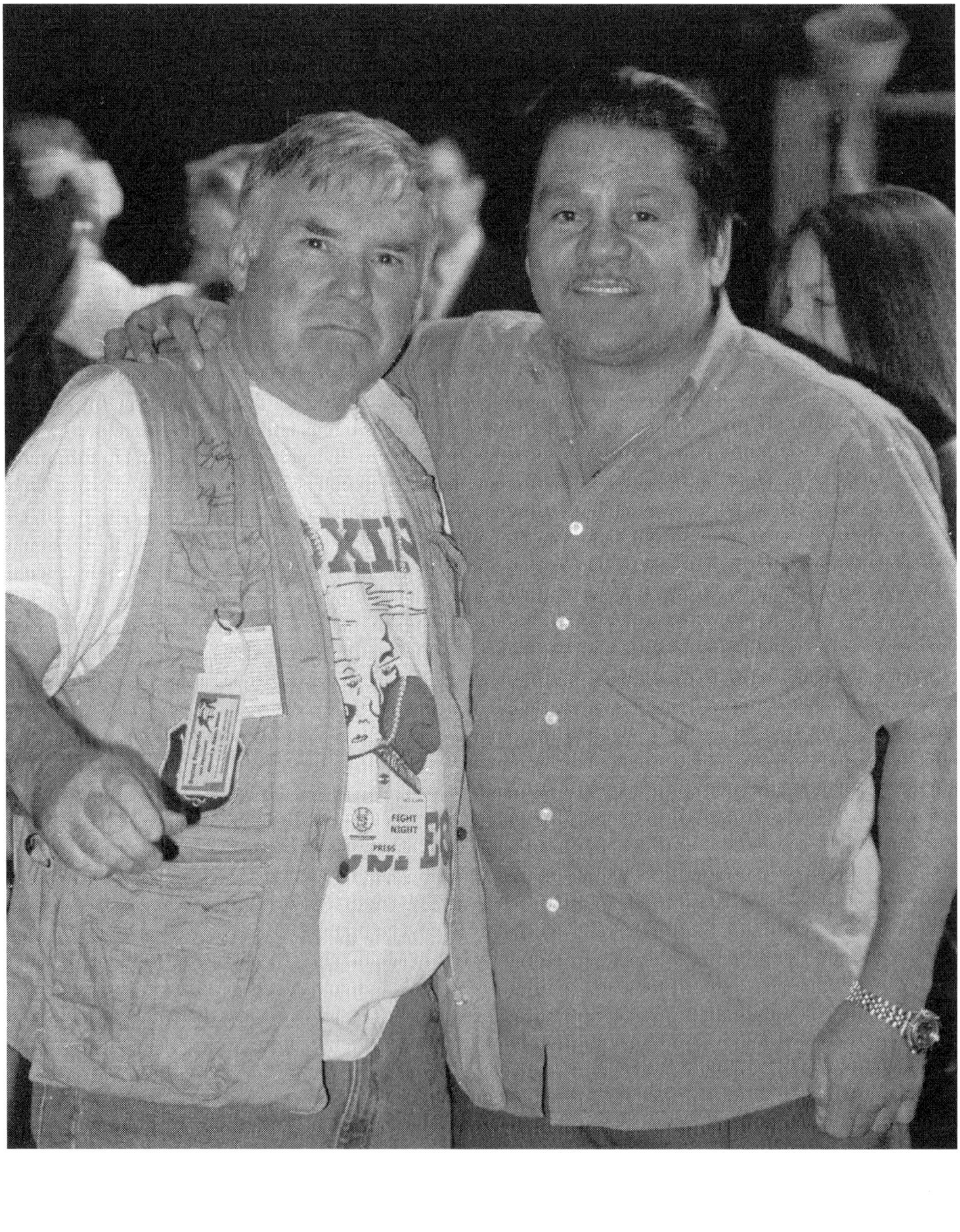
FIGHT
NIGHT
PRESS